D0272693

GIRL FRIDAY

GIRL FRIDAY

Joanna Lumley

BBC BOOKS

Picture Credits

BBC Books would like to thank the following for providing photographs and for permission to reproduce copyright material. While every effort has been made to trace and acknowledge all copyright holders, we would like to apologise should there have been any errors or omissions.

All photographs commissioned by BBC Books (**Brian Ritchie**) except: **Bruce Coleman** pages 21 (Dries van Zyl), 39 (C & S Hood), 57 (Alain Compost), 74 (Trevor Barrett) and 90 (Stephen Coyne); **Oxford Scientific Films** page 108 (Earth Scenes); **Laurence Dodds** pages 30, 117; **Mark Holding** pages 14, 16, 17, 23, 24/5, 26, 27, 43, 50, 53, 54, 58/59, 69, 71, 73, 82, 88. Endpapers and shell photographs by **David Ward**.

This book is published to accompany the programme entitled *Girl Friday* which was first broadcast in December 1994

Published by BBC Books, a division of BBC Enterprises Limited,

Woodlands, 80 Wood Lane

London W12 0TT

First published 1994

© Joanna Lumley 1994

The moral right of the author has been asserted.

ISBN 0 563 370718

Set in Baskerville by Selwood Systems, Midsomer Norton
Printed and bound in Great Britain by Butler & Tanner Ltd, Frome, Somerset
Colour separation by Radstock Repro, Midsomer Norton
Jacket printed by Lawrence Allen Ltd, Weston-super-Mare

Contents

Introduction

PAGE 8

I wonder what I've
let myself in for.

Day ... ONE

PAGE 14

First steps on
the desert island.

Day ... TWO

PAGE 26

Rain drives me to the
Albert Hall caves.

Day ... THREE

PAGE 36

'No crew!
What will happen?'

Day ... FOUR

PAGE 48

Foraging for food and
sulking on the beach.

Day ... FIVE

PAGE 60

I can stick it out tonight
but this is the end.

Day ... SIX

PAGE 72

The rainbows, turtles
and a perfect day.

Day ... SEVEN

PAGE 86

Dolphins at dawn and
daydreaming.

Day ... EIGHT

PAGE 98

This is the life
of the seraphim.

Day ... NINE

PAGE 114

Packing and
leaving forever.

Quotes **PAGE 127**

Acknowledgements

I would like to thank the BBC for dreaming up this ruse and making it happen; my typist Susan Proctor, Frank Phillips for his creative book design, my editor Nicky Copeland, and everyone who helped with the film and the book. However, my greatest debt of gratitude is to the crew who were there with me almost every day on the island. To some extent I suppose I owe them my life, as they could have just sailed off into the sunset and dropped the map overboard and I would have had to join the skeletons on Death Rock.

for Stevie and Jamie

Introduction

Would you have said no? Spend nine days on a desert island somewhere in the Indian Ocean; exist with a bare minimum of kit, spend much of your time alone, sleep rough, make do, get on with it?

I had some training with the Irish Guards in Surrey, but not quite enough to make me feel absolutely confident. There was so much to learn and so little time to do it in. I must have seen twelve different kinds of fire, ten ways to purify water, thirteen sorts of shelter. I was trying to remember how to do successful lashing, how to site a camp, and all the time puffing and panting after my new young soldier friends, who were incredibly kind and tolerant. Attitude and morale, I learnt, are vital – far more important than physique or health, although the two are connected. I thought how much fun it would be to have a companion on my adventure; someone to help lug trees about, someone to talk to, like my friends in the Irish Guards, someone with whom to share this thrilling experience. The Company Sergeant Major, Paddy, taught me more than I could ever have

learned from my SAS survival manual, and lent me his own Anaconda knife for the trip.

People thought I was mad, questioned my sanity, my husband, my family (who, knowing me as they do, smiled in resignation – they would have rather liked to have come too, I suspect). As the time got nearer, my nerve began to fail. The last entry in my diary, the day before the journey started, reads: 'Hope I survive all this.'

Here is what it was like.

OPPOSITE **Sitting between Jacko and Les with my brain moving rather slowly as the CSM, Paddy, lectures us.**
BELOW **Trying like fury to absorb all the rules about making fires, filtering water through socks and keeping morale high. Jacko and Les are ahead of the game.**
OVERLEAF **Tsarabajina from the south. 'Tsara' means 'good' or 'beautiful', 'bajina', means 'sands'. The high hill is where the fish eagle lives. (INSET) Dolphin Beach and the A-frame.**

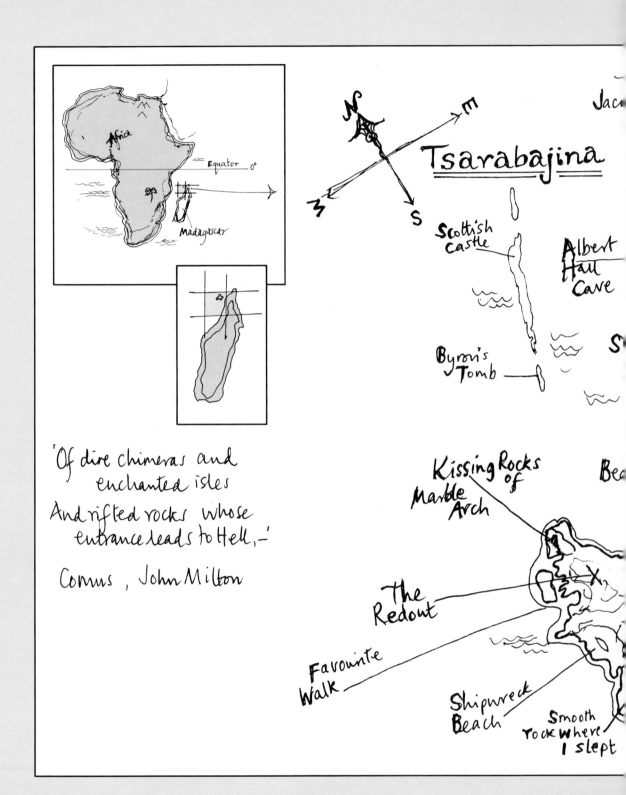

'Of dire chimeras and
    enchanted isles
And rifted rocks whose
    entrance leads to Hell,—'

Comus , John Milton

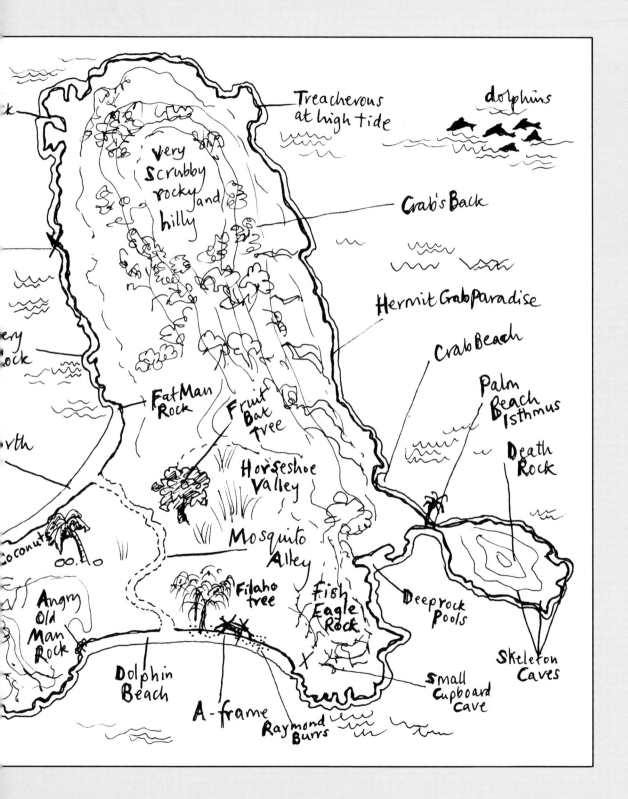

Day . .

This is what I can see from the helicopter: huge wrinkly blue sea, some vivid green patches where sandbanks almost push through the clear water, navy blue deeps, great coral reefs. There are some tiny islands which seem to be just rocks, tall, towering like little skyscrapers with brown sea birds wheeling around like titchy little gnats. I can't tell how big or small anything is, or how high we are. The engine is too loud to make conversation with the pilot, who only speaks French. I keep shouting 'This one? This one?' and he points ahead. There is the island, with a blaze of small white beaches and jungly interior. I am almost falling out of my seat trying to see the island's shape and remember it for my map drawing. She is like a crab, with pincers and a long hunched back, rocky edges and the little islands around her really are tiny. We are miles from the north-west coast of Madagascar, the horizon is hazy, the sea seems curved. I feel as though I am on a blind date – I want to love this place and be part of her at once. We are rushing down towards her, and I can see the trees clearly and the blistering beach and lazy rolling surf and now we're down, and I snatch up my ridiculous blue nylon rucksack with the clanging, dangling baked-bean tins and a roll of sacking stuffed into the straps and I push open the door and in the storm of sand and roaring of rotors I jump down and scuttle clear of the helicopter, which drones upwards and sheers off and is gone. Then there is silence.

Sweat is running down my neck and my hair is wet from the pressure cooker

As we land the heat makes the helicopter cabin feel like a pressure cooker.

14

...ONE

of that glass-bubble helicopter. The glare of the beach is so great that my eyes become Clive James-ish. I'm standing on shells and sand – the beach ends after about 40 yards in the jumble of low vegetation and wispy casuarina trees. Dead silence is broken by hoarse cawing from three or four black and white crows who, like the vultures in Disney's *Jungle Book*, will keep me company and comment on my every move. I'm trying to think 'my first steps on my desert island' but in fact I'm just tramping up the beach at 10 a.m. looking for shade and waiting for the dinghy that will bring the film crew from the boat.

There are some things I know already – we are in the Mitsio Archipelago, south of the Equator, due east of Mozambique and about thirty miles out to sea from Nosy Be, the nearest big island. The island has a name: Tsarabajina, meaning Beautiful Sands. She is visited by passing fishermen, but lives quite alone as she has no supply of water. I know she has bananas, pawpaws, berries, coconuts, sweet potatoes and probably much more if you're brave enough to try. I'm standing in the shade of the casuarina and banana leaves, slapping away at insect bites and waiting to fall in love.

To tell the truth I'm rather nervous about what I've got ahead of me. I've spent so much time saying 'Yes, yes, blah blah, I've slept rough, etc.', but I've never had to make my own shelter and hack up trees with this huge new knife which will hang by my side all day and lie by my face all night. I've made fires; but with matches and lighters and lots of us to feed it with branches – and, sure, I've slept out, but I've had sleeping bags and tents and clocks and thermos flasks. I've written books, but usually I have a chair at least and a table – and hours at night in peaceful brightly lit solitude, with coffee and cigarettes. Yes, I've drawn things, the odd birthday card, showing how something was made in a letter, but not work to be published from a pad crammed in with a mosquito net. In any case, I don't know how to draw as I wasn't taught, and I don't know how to write or act or, suffering catfish, survive on a desert island as *I haven't been taught* and have just got to sort of pick it up and make it up as I go along. That's exciting, but I'm smiling away in the shade and feeling a bit anxious. Also, I don't know how we're going to manage together, surviving *and* filming – it seems

ABOVE The island showing North Beach on the right and Death Rock like a claw on the left.
RIGHT My huge coarse whiskery sacking and the things I could bring.

one thing defeats the other. But the crew are arriving and I run from the insect shadows and we all gasp and laugh and wade out to unload the rubber boat. How quickly wet shirts and trousers a) don't matter, b) dry off. In the days that follow I stop being aware of wet and dry clothes – the shoes are the only things that make or break you.

2 knives and sharpening stone
2 empty bean tins to cook in
1 army mug
Sacking, size of large carpet
1 lb rice
Mosquito repellent
25-factor sun cream
Clothes: 1 pair of socks, 1 pair of
pants, 1 bra, 1 bathing dress,
shorts, short-sleeved shirt,
long-sleeved shirt, trousers,
3 sarongs, cap.
Drawing book, diary, pencils and pens.
Needles, string, fishing hooks and
nylon line, flint and striker, four
matches, three vegetable stock cubes.
Water-purifying tablets
Army-issue ladies' trainer shoes

On the ground I've spread out my allowance of things I could bring. They are all important on this trip, and have been chosen, it seems to me, with rather reckless abandon. I've also got a video camera and tripod, and the crew make me have a walkie-talkie. They are going to arrive and leave every day, and if the worst comes to the worst I shall be able to call them at night – my call sign is Friday and they are Lemur One to Lemur Six. I've got one bottle of water, the island to explore and a home to build. I've also got a tobacco tin prepared for me by the Irish Guards which contains pills, a button compass, a few bits of cotton wool and some of the smaller things listed above.

I said I haven't been taught how to survive but I have, in a very rapid way and, of course, on film. Before I came, I spent two days with the Irish Guards trying to pick up from their formidably all-encompassing course how to build ten sorts of fire, including earth ovens and smoke houses in which you could cure a shark; how to purify water through charcoal and old socks; how to build anything from a leaf-strewn lean-to to a fine little wooden hut with a bunk bed. I had a go at lashing great poles together and noticed with alarm how very puny my arms are and how nervous I am of cutting my hands off.

We set off round the island, travelling clockwise. In my excitement I forgot to take my button compass with me and so the all important decisions must be based on the position of the sun, which by now has got hold of a central position directly above us and is reducing extra flesh to ghee as it drills down in equatorial splendour. The island has a sort of rocky petticoat which means that, except for at very high tide, you can scramble the whole way round at sea level. She is quite stunningly lovely and completely wild. The sands aren't swept clean as they are outside grand hotels, and under the trees are twigs and sharp pine cones (Raymond Burrs), but where she feels like it, the beach is smoother than mother-of-pearl, and brighter than a ski slope. Sometimes you have to scramble, taking care not to slip – the rocks are covered with razor-edged oysters clammed shut when the sea is gone, and gaping with frilly black cutting lips when the clear water covers them. Rock pools are filled

A group of Raymond Burrs

with fish from aquariums, striped and spotted. There is a rocky outcrop joined by a sandy strip, then a beach covered with gigantic clam shells and crawling with huge hermit crabs: they have stolen shells the size of boxing gloves but if you pick them up they vanish inside them and play dead.

All the north side of the island is rocky, with caves; a long high-backed ridge of land with jagged cliffs covered with impenetrable low green scrub. I'm naming places as I go round, stupid names but anything that makes the place stick in my mind – Shell Beach, Palm Beach, the Jacuzzi (a large rock pool filled with hot salt water), Shower Rock and so on. There's one tremendous find – a huge dry cave, reached after some clambering over the sharp lava rocks. This is wonderful. Although the lower part is puddly from high water, inside there is a stone ledge and room for someone of four foot six, and that part is as dry as a bone. My friends, the Irish Guards, the Micks as they call themselves, told me to note carefully where wet weather shelters are as you never know when you'll need them. They had also instructed me to wear my rucksack at all times to collect things as I go – I've already started collecting driftwood for the fire and I leave a bundle of sticks and a terrifically heavy coconut in the cave. The cave is called the Albert Hall on account of its size. Right beside it is Shower Rock where a drizzle of water (rainwater?) trickles down from the overhanging cliff. It's so hot one could faint. Water, water: always remember to keep drinking, litres if possible. I've finished my fresh water and collect some drizzle from Shower Rock – it's opal and yellowy but will be perfect. The Micks said to purify all water as I have

ABOVE **The Madagascar fish eagle.
When he flies, his square tail is as white
as his chest.**

no time to be ill – two tablets for a litre, into the rucksack and so onwards.

Cutting back across the middle of the island seems a good idea. By this time my arms and legs are bare and the green jungle looks invitingly cool from the hot beach. There are coconut and banana palms, tall cutting grasses which look like bamboo crossed with sugar cane, and tall dark broad-leafed trees. We march through, sweating and struggling, and are at once covered with mosquito bites and another more ghastly stinging itching sensation which we all call sandflies but are insects from hell. Within minutes huge circular bites appear on faces, arms, legs, backs. We are driven nearly mad and scurry through, cursing and swearing, puce-faced and exhausted. The only remedy is the sea, and the first plunge into those waters is exquisite.

OPPOSITE **Finding the Albert Hall cave. I
hadn't yet registered the slashing ability
of the lava rocks.**

I have decided to build my shelter on this beach, the first beach. It runs east and west so I will see the dawn and the sunset, and at one end I have spotted a huge eagle wheeling about in the sky having a look at us. If this is the Madagascar fish eagle, I am very near paradise as there are apparently only eighty pairs left in the world. The crew have sloped off to have lunch under a tree. I keep apart and turn my mind away from food, which isn't hard. My appetite only appears when the sun has gone down. Kind visiting fishermen! In the undergrowth I spot several long heavy poles which they must have cut and prepared, but for what? Drying fish? Making temporary shelters?

The gorgeous shelter I have selected from my SAS survival handbook is the A-frame. It looks easy-ish and keeps me off the ground, away from Raymond Burrs and interested crabs, allows cool breezes to blow round it and affords some sort of potential for stowing away my measly but vital kit. I start off at a terrific rate, running about dragging these huge logs, and trying to lash them together in a tall X-shape. I am giddy with exhaustion and get slower and weedier by the second. The crew film on politely, although I'm sure they'd rather have a go at it themselves. Two wooden tripods and then the laborious stitching of the sacking: each stitch through four layers of fabric is an agony of effort and strength. My needle is the size of a submarine, the army string as thick as rope. Bits of sacking stick in my throat and the camera whirrs away as I struggle on, and the sun begins to set. Two poles inserted into the canvas tube form a stretcher, and then the stretcher, heavier than an iron gate, has to be jammed on to the shoulders of the tripod. In my handbook it says it takes two men to make the A-frame; and now the sun is going and I haven't got firewood, or done the lashings properly or put up the mosquito net. I don't know what to do about supper because it's so much trouble. The boat arrives, soft fat rubber boat, and the crew go as the sun dips down. It's beautiful but I'm in a flap as I haven't sorted out the video camera and am a complete amateur; I can't do my diary, I've done no drawings and the little boat pulls away, rubbery dark on the dark sea to the crew's ship. I jabber my piece to camera, and have to do it again as I forgot to plug in the microphone. I don't want any

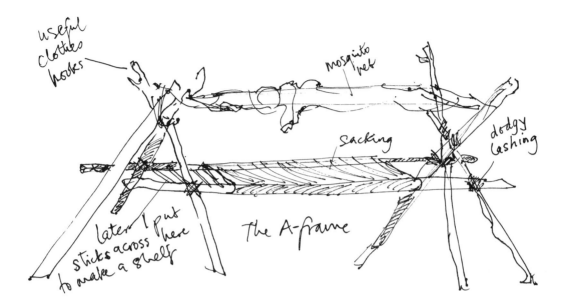

useful clothes hooks

mosquito net

Sacking

dodgy lashing

Later I put sticks across here to make a shelf

The A-frame

**Purple with exhaustion, trying
to make the stretcher part of the
A-frame. I am kneeling on
Raymond Burrs.**

supper now. The stars are very bright. My torch sweeping the beach picks up thousands of crabs: white ghost crabs who travel sideways at forty miles an hour and other larger brown chaps. When I walk, though, they part like the Red Sea, politely rushing out of the way. I never tread on the crabs. They are too quick and clever, so I can walk out easily with long, confident strides. Torch off: sea sounds, and if you look at the horizon, you can see the sand as clearly as in

The daylight dies swiftly here – minutes later it is night.

daylight. As the waves break there is a shimmering ripply gleam of light in the water. Phosphorus! I wade into the tepid water and by stroking my arms through the sea I send showers of stars from my fingers, like a tiny god.

W hat an extraordinary privilege: to wake up under a mosquito net on your own private beach and to see a slate-blue heron flying slowly past just above the water twenty feet away. I can't remember going to sleep last night. It was all I could do to climb on to my rather high bed in the inky darkness, and try to kick the sand off my wet feet. I didn't make a fire, or supper; I don't ever remember feeling so tired. All through the night I woke up and tried to get comfortable and listened to the sea and the night sounds and dozed off again.

I've made the A-frame stretcher a bit too narrow, so it will only be really comfortable when I can lie as straight as a rolling-pin without being afraid of knocking all my treasured kit down from the wobbly shelf I've propped at the foot end. The next task will be to make stick shelves at both ends, and I ought to try to make another one to go underneath to protect things from the rain. For the grim truth is that, despite the starry moonless night, today is thick and grey and drizzling. It's hot: but although I'm damp from the rain I'm still sweating. By the time the crew arrive it's raining fairly heavily and most of my precious things are squirreled away in a rocky fissure, which is nearly a small cave, at the

ABOVE **Checking the purified water by the Albert Hall; lugging water around in the rucksack becomes routine.**
OPPOSITE **Trying to get my first fire going in damp circumstances. (INSET) The rain depresses us all but the cameras have to keep turning.**

. . . TWO

end of the beach. The rain has both depressed and cheered me. My main anxiety about the island was how to get enough water, but this no longer seems a problem. The catering-size baked-bean billy-can propped on a rock is full in ten minutes. What is depressing is that in this grey fuggy light the island looks like Aldershot, and the jewel sea, the aquamarine LA swimming pool sea, looks rough and a bit like Hastings.

I make a fire in the small cave, which takes rather a long time especially as it's my first and the crew are watching. I think they hope that I'll be a worthy Girl Friday – I know they want me to succeed and not be completely cack-handed, but nevertheless a watched bean tin never boils and I seem to be snapping up whole armfuls of twigs to keep the licking petal of flame alive. The tea, when it's brewed, is acceptable – it has powdered milk and white sugar from my rations.

**The rocky fissure where my first cup of
tea was made is directly under the fish
eagle's favourite roost.**

In yesterday's list of permitted items, I forgot to mention that I was allowed a plastic sheet, an onion and an orange. I traded in the onion for tea bags and was given some army rations of sugar and whitener. I ate the orange this morning. The A-frame looks rather sad now that I've taken down the white mosquito net and left the little flimsy-looking sticks to the downpour. When I knew I was going to be allowed a mosquito net my heart leapt. As children my sister and I slept under them in the Far East; to me they symbolise security and happiness and make the dullest bedroll into a Turkish palace.

We can't go on crouching in this scabby crack in a dripping cliff, passing round a mug of cooling tea. The Albert Hall cave is the obvious and perfect answer. I'm going to leave a câche of things I won't need immediately (what? what on earth can I afford to be without?) in this rock cupboard and stamp through Mosquito Alley to the other side, the north side of Tsarabajina. This is exciting: I shall live in a cave on a desert island. That will look good in a book.

There are birds running about in the bushes, about the size of long-legged moorhens, clucking and crooning to themselves. If you stand still they come quite close, picking up leaves and looking for things, maybe crabs or insects or grasses. (If you stand still, the sandfly misery swarms over you like a cloud so keep walking, keep picking up sticks and shells, keep your spirits up even though the rain is now lashing through the dripping undergrowth and the islands in the sea have disappeared!) Lord! How treacherous the benign rocks have become. Holes to twist your ankle off are concealed under a hammering lid of brown liquid and a green slimy skin is covering everything. The tide is very high now: the last corner before the Shower Rock is frankly terrifying, with my ladies' trainers not gripping and huge waves roaring up to smash against my legs. By the time we reach the cave we're all wet through and even after such a short time we have started to notice blisters and rub-marks where sand and flakes of scaly rock have got between shoe and foot. The Albert Hall looks quite wonderful: very gloomy, it's true, but as dry as a catacomb except for the puddles at the entrance. There lies the bundle of dry sticks, there is the stony platform for the bed (not as smooth as I'd remembered ... but who could care less about that brick-sized outcrop in the middle). It's dry and safe and warm and when the fire gets going it will be peachy. Dark, certainly: but what a view! Framed by jagged lion's lips is a pot-holed apron of rocks soused by explosive waves and a raging grey sea beyond. I've always found storms comforting, particularly if you can watch them from a dry place.

There are several easy water catchment areas, i.e. drips, at the mouth of the cave which fill up the bean tin in thirty seconds, and as I decant the water into my bottle with half of it pouring down on to my feet, I can feel the first knots of normal behaviour beginning to loosen. It simply doesn't matter what gets wet as far as clothes go – it's so hot, and already my shorts are marked and charcoal-stained. Did I tell you about the other things I'm not allowed? No books to read, no soap or brush and comb, no toothbrush, no looking-glass. No music. No hand cream, towel or nail file, no scissors, no alcohol, no cigarettes. No sunglasses; in fact, nothing that might allow one to feel normal. This is a challenge. It will be very difficult not cleaning the teeth, a real problem for someone who cleans them

two or three times a day. The hair terrifies me – how will it be after nine days of tropical sun and salt water? I will look like a hay-net on legs. My nails, which I'd cut short before I came, are already black but I clean them with the pointed blade of my small knife.

Dear Irish Guards! Dear Paddy! I have been re-running in my head the jumble of information that assaulted me that day on the survival course. It's become terribly important to me not to let them down, and not to behave in a manner ill-fitting to the daughter of a Chindit. My father became one of Wingate's famous force in 1943 and spent six months miles behind the Japanese lines in Burma. Their movements were directed by wireless, and they were supplied and supported by air. The conditions were unspeakable. I can hardly be defeated by a spot of rain and not much food for just over a week. But it's not only that: I really want to make something of this strange time.

I am opening up the little green bananas I picked on my way here in Mosquito Alley and to my intense disappointment I find them as empty as an old pair of gardening gloves. They were never pollinated, they will never be bananas, there is nothing there. This is a blow: bananas were to be the mainstay of my diet. I did see a lime tree with small yellow limes which look excellent, so they'll make up for lack of bananas. I cut away at a fat piece of bamboo and fashion a sort of window box or shelf to keep things from getting lost. Even in the daylight it's easy to mislay vital things, like my firelighting flint. I was warned to keep important things like matches for a rainy day (huh!) so that, when one's spirits and energies are low, a match can bring instant light and warmth. Jamming a wooden pole across one of the rocky corners has created a clothes horse on which to hang my dripping shirt and shorts. The shoes are something else. They're mostly rubber and woven nylon, and wet or dry they stink of rotting fish. Fish feet. I take them off, knowing they won't dry out, and try to dry my feet using

---

The bananas look promising. I keep them in the cave even though they turn out to be empty, as their cheerful green colour brightens the gloom.

---

one of my cloths as a towel. I notice several cuts which gape wetly at me, filled with sand. Not wearing shoes in the cave is impossible, as the black lava rocks are like crumbling rusty razor blades to walk on. Fish feet on again. The idea of trenchfoot looms.

It's late afternoon and the crew are leaving. Yesterday and today they have brought over a packed lunch from the spivvy yacht, the ocean-going deep-sea diving cruise ship, where there is an excellent cook. From tomorrow onwards they will go back to the boat for three hours in the middle of the day as well, to eat properly, change camera batteries, and have a snooze or make phone calls. I shall not leave the island and I don't want to. Already there is a small bond building up between us, the island and me. I know that she becomes different with visitors; she takes a step backwards when there is a crowd of people and stands behind them, looking away and pretending not to listen. When they've gone, she moves closer again and looks me full in the face. I can't wait for people to leave me, as though there is a secret treat in store that I will get only when I'm alone. I sometimes feel this way when there's a ripe avocado waiting to be eaten at home, and I'm in a traffic jam. Whatever else may happen that gorgeous creamy avocado will be there – and here, whatever else happens, solitude will arrive in moments. I didn't really want to have the walkie-talkie link with the boat. I know I won't use it unless I'm made to; I don't like jawing on the telephone and I certainly wouldn't ring up for a chat out here. But if I fell over and snapped a limb, the jig would be up, no film and maybe a drifting corpse for the BBC, so it is a sensible plan. It's just that being sensible is sometimes a bore, a dampener on the spiky edges of fright and excitement.

I am, in the back of my head, a tiny bit afraid because like many people I've never been completely alone before and I wonder if I'll go mad with only my own thoughts in my head. Of course I've been 'alone' – but there have always been vestiges of other people's ideas in buildings, books, music. There's always the wireless, the television, newspapers with presenters and writers who look out at you, unseen, but appear to be speaking to you: 'Good evening. Here is the news', and even though you are

Sitting at the mouth of the cave, in the Lion's Lips, I watch blazing blue seas which inevitably turn to stormy grey.

The Cave fire

nothing to them and they don't know your name, you feel as though you are in conversation with them. Books, I think, will be the greatest loss to me on the island, but even as I write this I can't think what kind of book I would read right now. My mind can't settle on a book as the storm increases. I've stoked the fire up to a good blaze and somehow managed to balance a tripod of sticks over it from which dangles the billy-can with purified water beginning to boil. To make the vegetable stock cubes last I have put in only half a cube and about a third of a tin of water and a shoosh of rice from the packet – too much went in but the Micks said that high morale was one of the most important ingredients in survival and hot food was part of that. No food yesterday or today, except an orange, has given me an appetite. No spoon, no plate: to wash out a tin means going out into the rain which means walking on the rocks which means putting on the clammy stinking fish feet. You can't do anything quickly, or without thinking it out first (how to carry the torch, take off dry clothes before getting wet again, bring more wood up into the cave in case the monsoon lashes right inside). Supper is ready, and over the good sloshy stew of rice and water I squeeze a lime, which adds so much flavour that long after I return to England I find I am squeezing lemons and limes over everything.

The crew is waiting for me to call and say all is well, but the walkie-talkie won't transmit or receive from inside the cave. Palaver with fish feet, torch etc. and out on to the rocks in the gale. It's thrilling: the waves crashing under my feet, my torch presenting a flickering series of man-traps and jagged shadows. All I can say when I get through is, 'What's the time?' It's ten o'clock. The whole night to go through. More wood on the fire and spread out my bedding like an old dog, turning round and round trying to make the sacking and mosquito net into a bone-protecting mattress. I've slept on concrete floors in Borneo and the worst bits are shoulders and hip bones.

Luxury items already greatly desired: a towel and a pillow. I've smuggled on to the island several small treats, the first of which is a candle, as opposed to the Micks' nightlight. From a little niche in the cave wall it shines out, 'like a good deed in a naughty world'. I did *The Merchant of Venice* when I was ten and can remember some of Portia's lines. I can remember everything I learnt before I was twelve and nothing since then. The fire is about two feet away from the head end of my bed. It's stiflingly hot as the ceiling is so low. I feel completely safe and wide awake as though something hugely important is about to happen. Rain drumming down and the roaring sea and the crackling fire. I'll save the candle and lie in the darkness, trying to make my body fit in with the bumpy contours of my dog bed.

Day . . .

The night has been fantastic. I was so relieved to be safely protected from the storm that I kept waking up and thinking, 'I'm dry and I'm sleeping in a cave on a rocky shore on a deserted island miles from anywhere and it feels like home.' Then I'd doze off and wake up again to listen to the tremendous din outside. The sea practically came right up to the cave, but in the daylight there are just puddles and a crashing turquoise sea. From my bed, which is about five feet above the amphitheatre in the lower part of the cave, I can count eight or nine islands, which are just little rocky outcrops. Directly opposite me, due west where the sun sets, is Byron's Grave, and then a stream of small rocks to the right ending up with the Scottish Castle. These are just names that sprang to mind. I don't know why it's Byron's Grave: I just thought of him when I looked at the tombstone shape.

The bed was fairly comfortable but not the slithery green plastic sheet, nor the mosquito net which was like sleeping on a cheese grater. Terrible. The sacking, though, was excellent. I made an indifferent fire and a mug of tea and swept out the new bits of rock which seem to tumble ceaselessly on to the floor. I made a broom from the stuff that looks like sugar cane but isn't. Paddy said that it's very important to keep your camp as tidy and clean as possible, so I've graded the firewood from big logs to tiny kindling and prepared the next fire so that I'm

---

ABOVE **Some of the shells which have become an obsession with me. Spent half an hour spelling out my adopted name.**
OPPOSITE **Washing at Shower Rock takes all of thirty seconds.**

. . . THREE

ahead of the game. Long after dawn I was out on the promontory looking for the crew's rubber boat. The waves under a veil of drizzle looked threateningly high. When they didn't arrive I radioed them and found that they had had a terrifically choppy night on the pleasure steamer and that as the sea is still so rough they won't be able to land on the island at all today. First of all I think, 'No crew! What will happen?' Then comes a feeling rather like when the science block burns down and you won't have to hand in your chemistry prep which you haven't done. Freedom. So I roll up my sacking and tidy up my bed, scratch my head and re-tie the hair, buckle on my knives and put on my rucksack. Because the cave is about quarter of a mile from the nearest beach, I take everything with me, including my video camera, in case something of moment occurs and I can be the cub reporter. I will always wear my cap, vital protection against sun on the pate and raindrops in the eyes.

Round Slippery Rock I really do go carefully. Bright white foam is snazzing and frothing and the rocks are swarming with charming little rock hoppers, half-amphibian tadpoley fish, which flip and squibble away in shock waves as my Gulliver fish feet come tramping along. Just in front of the cave is a high deep rock pool which is replenished every day. As I peer in I see the long grey snout of a huge Moray eel, its tooth-filled jaws agape as it gulps slow mouthfuls of water, its eye watching me for a false move. Long after it's been left for

dead in the bottom of a boat, a Moray eel can snap off a man's hand. Its head is so large that its body must be eight or nine feet long, hidden in an underwater crevice. Everyone has said to me, 'Will you fish?' but I won't because I don't want to, I don't need to yet and I can't bear the idea of killing things. Fish seem to have as much right to stay alive as mice and warthogs. Never eat things with faces. Never put your arm into a rock pool in case the Moray eel takes your fingers off. Thank you.

Down on the beach, the sand is strewn with debris; sticks and shells and plastic bottles and flip-flop soles. All round the world every secret island where man has never trod is presented with daily deliveries of plastic trash. The soles give me the germ of an idea. If I could tie on the insoles from the fish feet, my feet would get dry and remain unslashed in the cave.

The shells seem much larger than usual, dredged up by the rough sea from the ocean bed. There are football-sized pieces of brain coral and flat giant mollusc shells the size of a side plate. No good for eating my watery rice stew, but useful for something. They are dark purpley-black outside and pure gleaming white inside, with a large indentation where the hawser-thick muscle attached the creature to its home. I find a huge perfect piece of feathery coral, white and orange, which will look lovely in the cave.

ABOVE **The moray eel lives like a dog in a watery kennel, spectacularly beautiful and dangerous.**
OPPOSITE **Often it's easier and more comfortable to draw standing up. I wish I had a camera with a Fleet Street zoom to capture the wildlife.**

Further on, I come across the top half of a crayfish or lobster, exquisitely marked in black and eau-de-nil; two sharp horns stick out, but the lobster has gone, been eaten or just died. I put all these treasures into my rucksack, along with a flat piece of wood which looks as though it had been a seat in a rowing boat. This will be comfortable by the fire. Anything smooth has become desirable, either for sitting on or using as a table or shelf.

The beach is at the north side of the island and is marked by important rocks at each end. One is Fat Man Rock, twelve feet high, like a statue of an American bootlegger, with a hat and badly cut suit. Beside him is a pale salt-bleached tree, smooth as a bone, weathered from being submerged twice a day. It has a natural curved seat. I can sit here and draw. Dum de dum de dum. I don't know what the time is and it doesn't matter as there's nothing for lunch and I've got firewood already. I film my rock and tree and go down the beach to film the Marble Arch Rock. There is something smooth on the sand – dark and slightly curved. It is a tray-sized piece of turtle shell. I sit down for a bit of a think. This is exciting because it means turtles are near here, but by the way the shell is squared off I fear this one has been eaten, chopped up by fishermen. In Madagascar it is illegal to buy or sell turtle products, but in every shop you can see turtle earrings, boxes and photograph frames. Either this turtle was eaten or caught for its shell. Poor turtle. The difficult problem to resolve is that the shell is undeniably beautiful, like ivory and leopard skin, but unless we leave these things on the living animals, we'll kill them all for ever. People sometimes say, 'Men have to earn a living', and sometimes 'It's the tradition to use rhino horn, and you mustn't interfere with traditions, religions, possible votes, etc.', but we're doomed unless they're protected by international law. I would flood the market with brilliant cheap plastic imitations (something good made from plastic) and knock the floor out of

First of all I named these rocks Marble Arch, but when I look again I can see that the two rocks are like bear-pigs, nose-to-nose, a mother and a baby; so they have become the Kissing Rocks of Marble Arch.

the market once and for ever. I pick up the shell and take it with me. Is this bad? I don't know. Am I wagging my finger at people and sinning at the same time?

There are scratchy little flowers, straw-coloured, all along the edge of the undergrowth. As I pick them the first sandfly attack of the day takes place. Marble Arch is composed of two rocks which look like fat bear-pigs kissing each other snoot-to-snoot with the baby on the right. Ducking down you can walk right through them. The rocks around here are veined with rusty seams like old corrugated tin sheets. I can see that the crew have managed to get on to a distant

rock, out of earshot. I'm not allowed field glasses (or a telescope or snorkelling equipment or a stills camera) but they seem to be doing some filming. I wave but can't tell if they are waving or drowning. I've been told to take my walkie-talkie with me wherever I go but it's too heavy and I don't want to talk to anyone while I'm engaged in vital beach-combing.

Above the Kissing Rocks of Marble Arch is a steep sandy hill covered with sighing casuarina trees. From here like a crow's nest I can see right round the corner to the room-sized sandy beaches and more rocks which form narrow corridors into which the sea roars like a train. There is a breeze up here, and bushes with tiny gooseberry-sized fruit. The way to test for poison is this: cut the fruit or vegetable and rub it on your arm. If it doesn't sting after fifteen minutes, rub it against your mouth. If that's okay, a little bit in the mouth, nibble nibble spit. If that seems safe, eat it. A quarter of an hour is supposed to elapse between each test, but I become impatient and wait only a minute. Most of the berries are green and unripe but the reddish ones taste sweet like rosehips. I eat three and collect ten for supper.

This high spot is called the Redout. I'm not sure if that is the appropriate word but the first name must be the fixed name. I would like to live up here in the heat, but today it's windy, and any kind of shelter would be rags in seconds. The undergrowth is full of sharp thorns and densely tangled undergrowth. Turning over a palm leaf reveals a mass of ants and millipedes. Insects are fine, but I'm pleased

OPPOSITE **Creeping through Marble Arch. I stood up too soon after this photograph was taken and nearly knocked my brains out**
RIGHT **The coconut palms on Sandfly Rise are depressingly tall as far as foraging goes.**

not to be sleeping in the interior with the rustling clicking leaves, and walkways for every kind of scorpion. There is only one kind of snake on the island apparently; a small boa constrictor, too small to do anything more than give my ankle a friendly squeeze. Snakes prefer continents. I march from the Redout in ten league strides down the soft sandy hill and set off back to the cave to get rid of the camera. Half-way down the beach I'm feeling exhausted. What's wrong? No water. I'm sweating pints and not drinking anything. I must remember to carry water with me. There's an old coconut shell, well washed by the waves, at my feet. I will make it into a ladle.

The weather is closing in again and it's only midday. Beyond the Albert Hall, the sky has gone buffalo grey and fat towers of rain are moving inexorably towards the island. I'm inside just in time, and spend half an hour putting my shells, coral and strawflowers around the scraggy cave walls. The mollusc shell I put as a sconce behind the candle, white side out so that it will bounce more light into the darkness in the evening. The little shells I put as markers, because when you have restricted light it's good to see where the walls are, and nice for your eyes to have something to fasten on in the gloom. By rigging up army string across a forked stick I have made a clothes line to put my wet clothes on. My sarongs look beautiful, with their patterns of butterflies and palm trees, and take away the feeling of living in a coal-mine. An idea the size of the Ritz comes to me as I take out my insoles to dry them. I could cut my bra up and bend the cups and stitch them on to the toes and make some kind of slipper. This is such a brainwave that I rig up the camera on the tripod and show how I will do it before I start. (Why am I so anxious to prove that I'm doing these things myself? I suppose because before I left everyone said, 'Oh well, you'll have food and sleep on the boat with the crew and use the telephone and wash your hair.' But it's so remarkable and tough here that I couldn't bear it if people thought I was skiving. The crew offered me food yesterday, but of course I didn't take it, nor shall I. I've got to do this thing properly, even if I'm the only one who knows.)

In my Irish Guards tin is a needle and some very strong nylon thread. Using my small knife, I cut the bra exactly in half and work out how to make the shoes strong enough to contain a foot. There is only so much thread. I unreel it and cut that in half too, so each foot will be equal. Once I have put the bra to its insole, it's as if the Tailor of Gloucester himself had designed it. The cup, folded over, covers my toes – the sides go down the side, the straps form adjustable thongs to tighten or loosen the slipper. I stitch as if my career depended on it, using a small shell as a thimble. The rain has made a waterfall curtain at the Lion's Lips, the mouth of the cave, and the ceaseless dripping and pattering is very soothing. As I'm working my brain begins to go inwards. All my thoughts are about here and now – I have no plans but to make these shoes. No one can reach me by letter or telephone. I switch off my walkie-talkie so even the crew can't contact me.

When I finish the sewing, the espadrilles are ready to put on. They are completely perfect, an unbelievable and dazzling achievement and I am so proud I can hardly stop looking at them. I walk gingerly two or three steps and the misery of cave-foot is gone for ever. I want to keep them clean till the crew sees them so I put them in a niche, like little *broderie anglaise* wedding shoes. I'll start

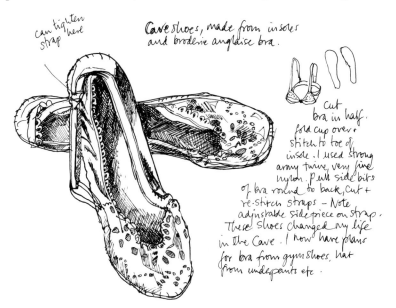

can tighten strap here

Cave shoes, made from insoles and broderie anglaise bra.

Cut bra in half. fold cup over + stitch to toe of insole. I used strong army twine, very fine nylon. Pull side bits of bra round to back, cut + re-stitch straps – Note adjustable side piece on strap. These shoes changed my life in the Cave. I now have plans for bra from gym shoes, hat from underpants etc.

on my coconut shell, boring two holes through which to poke a sharpened stick. All I want to do is make tiny improvements and do things with my hands. Therapy for the partially talented. If I had time I'd carve wooden birds, mix paint, make a statue. If you're not setting snares and skinning weasels you've got wild-man time to do things like look at clouds and plait grass.

While I'm dreaming, it suddenly becomes sunset time and a red slit appears above Byron's Grave showing the sun just above the horizon and night waiting in the wings. Help! I haven't prepared for the evening; put away my sewing things, measured the rice, sharpened my knives, opened up my bedding. To keep my bra-shoes clean, I squelch about in the fish feet which, without insoles, are too big (blisters in waiting). The sun goes down like the *Lusitania*, leaving a scarlet chariot of clouds shaped like swans which fade to grey and vanish. A rush of depression comes as the light goes. 'Rage, rage against the dying of the light.' The day has gone and I haven't written a word yet, and supper must be cooked in its black devil can. How am I to draw? If it's raining outside and dark inside, how can I draw? After ten minutes a good little fire is going and I put in a small

This is my soup plate and spoon. Some of the larger shells have become porous and rice stew leaks out, so I have small helpings from a small shell.

shell of rice and a bit of sweaty vegetable cube. The rice never cooks, so I eat it with hard centres and lime squeezed over. It's all eaten in three minutes. I forgot to get the red berries out of the rucksack so they're squashed under shells but I eat them, sand and all, in one mouthful. And carrot. I was allowed a carrot, just one, and was saving it for a rainy day, for a monsoon day, but tonight I had one bite and put it back in its shell. I can hardly bear to rig up the video camera as my mind has shut down and my eyes don't blink any more. I will die of tiredness. How can I be so tired? I will call for contraband tomorrow, cigarettes and alcohol. That's it! Coffee! At home, I live on coffee and a fag. When I scratch my head, great scabs seem to have formed quite painlessly, but it turns out to bits of the shaley cave roof which get stuck there every time I bang

my head. In my brain is Liu's aria from *Turandot*: 'Signore, ascolta!' 'Listen to me, my Lord', but I don't know the words or, upon examination, the tune.

Day . .

Drip drip drip. I can't tell if that's rain or the endless drizzling waterfall. I've been awake half the night trying to lie somehow on these wicked hateful rocks. There's no possibility of stretching out, or lying flat. All I want is to collapse on to a smooth flat anything, an ironing board or station platform. As dawn comes up, I remember the feeling of dread from my first year at boarding school when we'd arrived home from Malaya. There were grey, antiseptic smells and boiled cabbage, linoleum, arithmetic lessons with long division, hard squeaking floors and a feeling of being an alien. I didn't know catch-words from comedy shows on the wireless, and I feared assembly and the *Marche Militaire* on the upright piano which meant we must march like little soldiers to our classrooms. I would have preferred to have been at home, with our excellent way of living; walking with the dog, reading, playing, mucking around.

Now I'm trapped, humourless and sour, with no sleep in this dreadful cave. I daren't say that aloud: the cave can hear and it's been an enormous boon, kindly and welcoming like un-favourite relations. I'm exaggerating everything, saying it's gorgeous, fantastic, a huge treat, excellent, when in fact I'm kippered from the smoke, wet through with rotting cut feet and stinking hair and feeling sullen and mutinous. I can't believe that this is what was intended when the idea of this film

Trying to remember what it feels like to sit on something comfortable. I am gazing at Byron's Grave, just out of sight.

...*FOUR*

came up: an angry middle-aged bagwoman in a dark cave doing nothing and complaining. I shall have to pull myself together. But it is the cave's fault. If I could see the sky and the birds and hear trees rustling it would be a real, lovely world. If I could watch the tide move up and down the smooth beach instead of waiting for the smash crash of high tide thumping the great sea all over the deck. And the dripping must stop. Today, when I'm outside, it's not raining at all but in the cave it is eternal rain in eternal night; like the end of the world when the bomb has fallen and there's no point in living. Get a grip, woman. All will be well. The crew will come and we'll do some filming.

The idea is to go foraging for food today. I'm going to try and hunt down some sweet potatoes and a thing called a Malgache cabbage; the leaves of each are imprinted in my memory from pre-trip swotting. There should be more than rice to eat, rice with limes. Hmm. Last night's supper would have fitted into one cupped hand, but again I'm not hungry. If I try to think of food, all I come up with is very salty crisps and peanuts. Not wildly ambitious. Could mean I'm short on salt. But here's the crew! Lovely, clever, laughing, fit, competent brave crew! And good grief, they have brought me a metal thermos filled with coffee. They are demi-gods, mind-readers. They were anxious about me and I had been anxious about them. I would prefer any cave or dark pit to rolling about on the high seas in a luxury diving boat. We've missed a day's filming (but hang on, this is a kind of documentary: if nothing happened, nothing happened. Ah, but you have to FILM nothing happening) so we must crack on.

These vegetables won't be found beside the beaches – we'll have to go into the interior. On with trousers and long-sleeved shirt, the anti-insect kit. We all spray ourselves till we gleam and splutter with insect repellent. Now I would like to tell you about something else I smuggled on to the island, which I bought from a woman on the big island Nosy Be, before I came here in the helicopter. Coconut oil, in a brown cough mixture bottle, with no label, made up by her. Her name is Lala, Madame Lala I call her, and she was a kind chattering little person who had thirteen children and another on the way.

She told me the oil is an excellent mosquito repellent, and good for the hair too, so I am glistening now with Madame Lala's patent Acme coconut oil. Some of this has got on to my drawing book but that can't be helped. Today I'm carrying my opal purified water too, and this morning I sharpened my knives the way Paddy had told me, so I can cut and dig anything.

We tromp off over the rocks down to the North Beach, over Sandfly Rise into the damp green jungle. The first thing is how happy we are to be away from the stony hardness of the Albert Hall. The second is we are bitten, at once, from head to heel and the third is that I have been walking past Malgache cabbages without focusing on them. They have tall, rather elegant leopard-spotted stems supporting a wide attractive ferny leaf. The cabbage is underground. I've no idea what it looks like but I hack down the stem and start digging in a wide circle. After a few minutes I come across a pale bald monk's tonsure, a smooth turnip

RIGHT **Deep in the ground under this gorgeous foliage lurks the Malgache cabbage. This is right at the beginning of Mosquito Alley, not far from the fruit bats' tree.**
OPPOSITE **The fronds on this palm leaf are soft and bendy – I plait it into a nice but useless mat, which later becomes a bed-head.**

thing. It takes a while to dig out; I am watched by the whirring camera and the crew slapping mosquitoes on their arms. Up it comes: it is the size of a grapefruit, thickly covered with mud and bearing a crown of roots. General satisfaction all round. I clean the mud off my blade and put the thing into my rucksack. The sweet potatoes grow underground too, and forty yards further on I find their vine, which looks like a morning glory. You feel your way along the stem, like a game at a party, until the vine goes under the earth and there you will find gold. I start digging: in my mind's eye I can see the large pinkish torpedo-shaped potatoes at Sainsbury's, which are extremely good roasted or boiled or even baked. I could bake one of these huge pink chaps and have a vast excellent supper. Dig, dig ... but what's this? What is this scrawny little rooty parsnip? 'Are all thy conquests, glories, triumphs, spoils shrunk to this little measure?' Is it even a sweet potato at all? I will test it out tonight before I dig up any more, before the crew and I run mad driven by the stinging itching plague of sandflies.

High above us in the stifling interior is a hilly horseshoe covered with scrub and banana trees and far above is the fish eagle on a thermal, keeping an eye on us. It must be quite a thing for the birds and animals (what animals?) to be invaded by eight people, one of whom stays all the time. No wonder they watch us covertly; there is no telling what man will get up to. We move very quickly on through Mosquito Alley. The wet lalang, the cutting grass I remember from Malaya, snarls up into ropes round our ankles and cuts our legs.

I pick up some more yellow limes which have fallen down in last night's rain.

I am now devoted to these limes. What I'd really love would be a cos lettuce or a head of chicory or an apple – anything that goes crunch. Furtively I rub my shirt tail over my teeth. As soon as you cannot see yourself, you lose interest in your appearance. Maybe it's because women are under such pressure to look attractive that we feel the strain more. Certainly many men I've met clearly couldn't give a fig what they look like, and get away with it. Maybe it's just because it's part of my job to look ... what? Well, clean and fashionable and suitably dressed and *not old*, and not fat or grey or spotty. Men can be all those things and be loved passionately by kind and great-hearted women. But we women are somehow always made to feel self-conscious, from magazine articles called 'What do you hate about your body' to spiteful photographs of First Ladies in the Wrong Coloured Jacket. Give me strength. Here it's all gone, it has vanished away without a struggle straight down the plughole. The crew treat me like a man and, apart from commenting on bites ('Your whole back is covered'), we don't talk about the way we look, except for sunburn ('You've really caught it on your ears'). Not much chance of sunburn it would seem – and yet when the sun sears through the smoggy sky we are at once roasting like cooked meat.

Mosquito Alley leads past the moorhens' home under the shade of scratchy bushes. In the bloom you can see them with their chestnut fronts and white necks, unafraid and impatient for us to stand still or move on so they can get on with their leaf-turning. Through the casuarina trees and on to the beach. There is the forlorn A-frame standing on a drift of Raymond Burrs and twigs, and there, in the sea fifty yards out, a large school of dolphins. This is magic. Dolphins are well known for the effect they can transmit over distances to people watching. They are the ancient symbol of music and happiness and the Queen of the Minoans had them painted in a frieze around her bedroom walls in the palace at Knossos on Crete. We stand and stare, all dreaming of swimming with them. They are leaping and rolling and jumping in pairs. We look like pilgrims being blessed by the Pope, with shining eyes and open mouths. Half the crew are deep-sea divers; they may have a chance to get near them. Dolphins never work to

plan and are completely unpredictable. In the days that follow, and we see them every day, they always appear at different times. The first indication that they're around is a flurry of water and a consternation of fishes leaping and churning the surface as the dolphins move in, underwater, dawdee dawdee like Jaws, to chase them. Some fish fly from the sea as if they had been fired by a bow, thtoom! straight out like arrows. Dolphins eat fish, you could eat fish. Ah, but I eat Malgache cabbage and limes, I don't need fish. Yet. The A-frame beach is called Dolphin Beach now.

The rubber dinghy has come to get the crew for lunch on the yacht, and I wave goodbye to them for three hours (hours? what hours?) and trudge back to sit and think on a sopping wet tree trunk that has appeared from the sea. I'm now talking to myself out loud with great ease. A lecture must be delivered on

The abandoned A-frame under its filaho tree. I can't wait to get back to it.

not sulking and doing things with bad grace. When people have said to me, 'Oh, let yourself go, say what you like, it'll do you good', and I do, I always regret it. I hate saying and doing things that you can't undo or take back. They hang for ever like death masks on the walls of your bedroom, like Turandot's slain suitors, reproaching you. Nothing can unsay something said. (I still can't sing Liu's aria but now I can hear it right through in my head. I wish I could sing like a diva.) So I jam myself against the wet log and my funny old blue rucksack (not mine: I wanted to take an earth-coloured one) has become a good comfortable pillow. I look at the islands; sea birds, frigate and boobys I think, and the heron, all get on with their flying, and the crabs come out of their holes and start collecting food again.

He saw the April noon on his books aglow,
The wistaria trailing in at the window wide;
He heard his father's voice from the terrace below
Calling him down to ride.

In the most stupendous temper sulk: a very charmless picture. When I stopped brooding I found a lovely shell under my hand.

In my head I see the house and our garden in spring, and the sound of the piano and the little cat catching gnats. It's like watching a film. I'm not homesick, I just want to watch this film. When I wake up there is a beautiful shell just under my  hand and three white fishes with black forked tails like swallows leap in unison from the shallow waves.

When the crew returns, we trudge back to the Albert Hall. On the way I pick up a huge fallen coconut palm from under its tree. I shall have a go at making a mat, copied from memory of matting I've seen before in these Indian Ocean islands. I can't quiet remember how it goes but it shouldn't be difficult. Then at least I'll have a smooth mat. As we climb round Slippery Rock the rain clouds form up from the north and I can feel the spirits going zooming down to zero. There are many deep puddles outside to wash the vegetables in so I bring my rowing-boat seat out of the cave and sit on the dagger rocks and scrape away with my knives. First the parsnip-potato, which, when clean looks about as big as a finger, scrubbed and chopped into neat circles. Then the Malgache cabbage which, when washed, is a ghastly china white and smooth as a billiard ball. This can't be right. It must be cut into thin slices, dried for twelve hours and then boiled for sixty minutes. I cut it on the rowing-boat seat, as you must never use your knife against rock or you'll ruin it. By the time the cabbage is lying there in moon-white circles my hands are stinging, really stinging. I spread the slices on a banana leaf and put them by the Lion's Lips, just out of the rain. The place where my hand touched my forehead has started stinging too. This is the most elementary part of the poison test, and the Malgache cabbage, as far as I'm concerned, is lethally dangerous. I'll go through the motions of preparing it, but I'm not mad, I'm not going to eat one bit of this poisonous orb.

We slog back to North Beach to do some beach-combing. The crew pick up shells, and I pick up wood which I can dry out by the fire. I'm getting better at recognizing good kindling. Bamboo is very smoky and doesn't hold the flame, but there is a nice red stick which when split has a dry fire-friendly inside and I collect as many as I can hold. Suddenly we see faintly in the sand the distinctive paw prints of a cat. They are cat's footmarks. There is a cat on the island! This is tremendous. I shall have a friend to watch out for, although I've got nothing to offer it to eat. It must have come with the fishermen and been left behind, which is how cats got all round the world in the first place: by jumping ship. And just a few paces further on are fresh marks, maybe only a day old, of a heavy flat body with sharp feet at either side, leading to and from the sea. A huge turtle had come up to lay her eggs here on North Beach, where I first found the piece of turtle shell. We find a four-foot shallow hole, which might be her decoy nest. The excitement of seeing a turtle fills us all with renewed hope. The island has so many secrets and all we have filmed so far are poisonous vegetables and insect bites.

The crew would like to film my cave. Heavens to Betsy! Thank goodness I swept, tidied and decorated it yesterday. They'd also like to film my fire so I bustle about puffing into the embers and get a good fire going. They're not ready to film yet so I feed it more wood. And even more. Now they'd like higher flames – there! And my billy-can is bubbling away and the cave looks peachy. In the evening, red light flares into the darkest crevices of the cave and it looks rather like a nightclub on a summer's morning – out of place and rather tame. I show the camera my kitchen and wardrobe and store cupboard and shelves and my neat uncomfortable bed and my cave shoes.

The whole thing is a huge success but the sun sinks, and the bungy rubber boat biffs on to the far beach and in minutes the crew have gone, leaving me with an orange and two cigarettes. The fire dies completely as I stand on the promontory to wave goodbye, but the sunset is so strong, scarlet and blue that I sit on the rocks for a bit, staring. The heron flies by very slowly, looking sideways at me and cocking his head. Then, going in the other direction, a fruit bat, a flying fox, comes past so close with huge slowly flapping umbrella wings and a ginger foxy face. They're checking me out. I try to get the fire going again: by the time I've got a small flame, and am purple and sweating from blowing on the embers, the stars have come out. A fire has to be tempted, like feeding a sick child.

It's no use suddenly dumping armfuls of dry wood on to a candle-sized flame. You must make little attractive morsels, sometimes teasing the wood into shavings like wooden Christmas trees; 'Would you like this? No? Then try some of this', very gently and the fire likes some bits and not others: and soon you're over the terrible fever and colour returns to the pale little cheeks and the patient is running round the sickroom.

I cook some rice and the sweet potato button-sized segments in the tin from hell, but not for long enough; and when I eat the grey waxy lumps they're fine

The fruit bats or flying foxes taking the evening air. Sometimes they come so close to look at me that I can almost count their whiskers.

but a bit chewy. My spoon is a lovely pink and yellow shell, my plate a white clam model. The food is disgusting but redeemed by the limes. I smoke a cigarette and drink some whisky, a thimbleful, that I smuggled on in a miniature honey pot, and feel a hell of a tearaway. Tonight I shall wear my rucksack to bed to protect my back from the boulders.

**Watching the clouds at sunset over
Byron's Grave. Going back into the cave
after this is jaw-clenchingly sad.**

ast night there was the most phenomenal storm. B-movie rain lashed this way and that as the winds changed, and there was thunder like amateur dramatics and lightning, both forked and sheet, blazing and crackling. I lay like a tramp with my rucksack jammed under me watching the spectacle through the cave mouth. The waves were colossal, jagged grey mountains of water smacking down and exploding on the rocks. I feared for my poor crew, pitching and tossing on the stormy deep or, in this case, stormy coral reefs. The liner de luxe moves round the island in bad weather, trying to find a safe mooring in the lee of the island. I can't think where they crept off to last night; probably had to ride out the storm further out to sea. Oh, hateful seasickness. Our family travelled regularly on troopships to the Far East and back: the Bay of Biscay was the end of my young life each time we went through, rolling on the swell, seeing from the portholes only sea this moment, and only sky the next.

Before they went yesterday the crew made me take a watch to wear, a green and black plastic waterproof one which I forget to look at. In my fitful bouts of sleep I had just come to the edge of a dream when I was jolted awake by the

Sometimes the best moments for drawing are before the crew arrives. The blue heron watched me sketching this empty crab shell.

...*FIVE*

most incredible trumpeting roar, a sound like a train hurtling over me from inside the cave, so loud that my insides quivered and I couldn't feel my arms and legs. My eyes were staring wide and I was turned to stone by the sheer stupendous volume of the sound. It rolled out of the Lion's Lips and was gone in about six seconds. Maybe a thunderbolt had hit the cave or lightning had struck the cliff above me. In any case, I shook for minutes, not really from fear, more in excitement; the rocks under me were humming and throbbing too, and then it was gone and the storm raged on. I switched on my miner's lamp torch that I wear on my forehead and saw the time: 3.24 a.m. Dawn in about two hours. Like my appetite, sleep seems to have deserted me. I lit my candle like this: a little piece of cotton wool soaked with a quick burst of insect repellent, scrape, rasp with the flint then just catch the flame with the nightlight's wick. I started a very small fire for comfort, and sat trying to dry my feet which have become damp and porous like pale sponges. I wish I could go about barefoot and harden up the soles of my feet. They look as though I've been in the bath too long, wrinkly and soft. I could cut slices off them. If I walked on the cave floor barefoot now I think they'd just tear and fall off. I would give anything to have dry feet; even holding them in front of the fire only heats them up and doesn't dry them.

I run down to greet the crew on the North Beach. It's two hours after dawn. There are fresh turtle tracks so she must have come back last night. We must try to camp out if this dreadful weather ever lets us, and film her surreptitiously. We are seeing these dolphins, eagles and fruit bats (whose Latin name is *Pteropus vampyrus*), herons and crabs but are we filming them? Will we ever see the island cat? We climb to the hill above the cave, clambering and clawing our way over boulders. From here looking north to the main islands

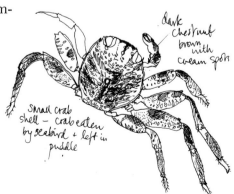

dark chestnut brown with cream spots

Small crab shell – crab eaten by seabird + left in puddle

OVERLEAF **Beyond the rocky reefs are three of the Four Brothers, Les Quatre Frères. I'm wearing 'interior' clothing as I've just meandered through Mosquito Alley and had to cover up.**

...FIVE

most incredible trumpeting roar, a sound like a train hurtling over me from inside the cave, so loud that my insides quivered and I couldn't feel my arms and legs. My eyes were staring wide and I was turned to stone by the sheer stupendous volume of the sound. It rolled out of the Lion's Lips and was gone in about six seconds. Maybe a thunderbolt had hit the cave or lightning had struck the cliff above me. In any case, I shook for minutes, not really from fear, more in excitement; the rocks under me were humming and throbbing too, and then it was gone and the storm raged on. I switched on my miner's lamp torch that I wear on my forehead and saw the time: 3.24 a.m. Dawn in about two hours. Like my appetite, sleep seems to have deserted me. I lit my candle like this: a little piece of cotton wool soaked with a quick burst of insect repellent, scrape, rasp with the flint then just catch the flame with the nightlight's wick. I started a very small fire for comfort, and sat trying to dry my feet which have become damp and porous like pale sponges. I wish I could go about barefoot and harden up the soles of my feet. They look as though I've been in the bath too long, wrinkly and soft. I could cut slices off them. If I walked on the cave floor barefoot now I think they'd just tear and fall off. I would give anything to have dry feet; even holding them in front of the fire only heats them up and doesn't dry them.

I run down to greet the crew on the North Beach. It's two hours after dawn. There are fresh turtle tracks so she must have come back last night. We must try to camp out if this dreadful weather ever lets us, and film her surreptitiously. We are seeing these dolphins, eagles and fruit bats (whose Latin name is *Pteropus vampyrus*), herons and crabs but are we filming them? Will we ever see the island cat? We climb to the hill above the cave, clambering and clawing our way over boulders. From here looking north to the main islands

OVERLEAF **Beyond the rocky reefs are three of the Four Brothers, Les Quatre Frères. I'm wearing 'interior' clothing as I've just meandered through Mosquito Alley and had to cover up.**

dark chestnut brown with cream spots

Small crab shell – crab eaten by seabird + left in puddle.

of the Mitsio Archipelago you can see where the weather comes and goes. It's sunny but there's a wild changeable feeling in the air. I must leave the cave soon. Even if I sleep in a tree I've got to be in the fresh air again.

I've made a nice little drawing of a crab shell, dropped by a gull. Just sitting and drawing is a pleasure. There's no time to prepare or make sketches, just seize a black ink pen and copy down what you see. Seeing is the important part of drawing. If you can train yourself to look at things and see them exactly as they are and to be truthful about light and shade you get something recognisable. I wish I were an artist. I wish I had been allowed coloured chalks or watercolours in the island but heigh ho: and I'd never have had the time. If I could get free from my life I could draw and paint all the time and maybe get better at it. At home, every day brings a fresh sack of letters and requests, bikes with deliveries, telephone calls; and there's no time to develop any of the ideas bubbling away in my brain, as, even if I can't do the things people want me to do, they have to be written back to, and every letter has to start, 'I'm so sorry ...', so that each day brings with it a sense of negativity. But here on Tsarabajina, pronounced incidentally *Tsara-badzina*, I am completely free for the first time since I was in a pushchair. Also no grass needs cutting; no shops, parking tickets, police sirens, no news of death and horrors, no newspaper photographs of burned soldiers and slaughtered civilians. In my present state of reduced thinking capacity, I don't think about the world at all, only the island. The island is my world.

Last night's fires have consumed all my firewood and I still haven't collected nearly enough shells. Plod plod, stoop, inspect, shuffle, plod. I've started to walk like an old woman. Zing has left my step, my carcase is zing-free. Bits of string hang from my waist, ready to tie up twigs. My eyes don't seem to need sunglasses. Hours pass easily when you're beach-combing. One of the crew has got a large green carrier bag which I want very badly, so I take it. It's only plastic but it is valuable beyond pearls. In it I put my drawing things so they can inhabit the rucksack with the kindling wood and not get too damaged. Funny how tiny things assume great importance ('strange how potent cheap music is'). Every time

Collecting firewood. Sometimes I leave it in bundles to collect later, if I remember where I dumped it.

I've travelled to poorer countries than Britain – Eritrea, Hunza, Sarawak, Syria – I give presents in plastic carrier bags which are received with almost as much pleasure as the things inside. In London, bags are thrown to blow about the streets of Brixton and Stockwell. We're poor in a different way in Britain.

Another lightbulb wheeze has struck me. As it looks from the sky as if I'll have to spend a fourth night in the cave, the notion of a mattress has formed in my narrow ape-like brow. There is the huge piece of sacking which on its own is too thin to prevent Night-time Boulder misery. But stuffed with grass ...! I march the crew down to Mosquito Alley with my big knife at the ready. Fern or bracken would have been ideal but I have to make do with the razor-sharp lalang. It's very tough and resistant to my scything efforts and I end up by yanking handfuls out: tiny thorns stick in my palms, feather-fine and almost invisible. If I had glasses I could see to tweak them out (if I had tweezers). This is an exhausting exercise and the sun suddenly steps out from behind the clouds like the door of a furnace being flung open. We are dizzy with dehydration and drink all our water. The crew give me some of theirs and also a Rehidrat tablet which replaces lost salts and minerals. I feel like a Japanese paper flower placed in water: blooming, restored, all-powerful.

Under the shade of the huge-leafed trees there are freshly gobbled red fruit stones, about the size of a large almond. Up above us, like fat umbrellas, hang the fruit bats. Their favourite time for flying in Horseshoe Valley is at about four o'clock, when they dawdle about like small Draculas, flapping into the trees and, as they land, turning upside down and resettling to sleep. As they fly you can see their sharp toes on the end of their wide membranous black wings. There is a scarlet bird, the red fody, as tiny as a finch, coloured dayglo crimson. Butterflies follow us around, settling on the crew's coloured shirts and the bright blue of my rucksack. There is a really weeny little bird, the suimanga sunbird, with a curved beak the size of a darning needle, nipping about on the tree trunks, and hornets drone and buzz out of the bushes. When you stand still the place is alive with creatures. Flowers topple and tumble; pink orchids growing in rocky caves, yellow floppy blooms, small mauve irises. I wish I had a bird book, flower book, geological book. I must make a proper map of the island, climb trees and cliffs and note the wind direction. If only we didn't have to film ... Sisal grows here in great clumps of sharp dark green spears. I know how to beat the leaves till the flesh falls away and you're left with the fibre. I could make sisal carpets, or plait up some string or make a good thick rope. If I had time I'd make a rope ladder or a tree house up with the fruit bats.

ABOVE LEFT AND RIGHT **In Horseshoe Valley
I am watched cutting lalang by the
fish eagle who I can see circling above
me on a thermal.**
OPPOSITE **It's very easy to get used to
dozing on tree trunks in the midday sun.**

Something has started to happen, a kind of amnesia which gets hold of my mouth in the middle of a sentence and makes my mind blank. Sometimes I can't tell if I'm merely thinking things or actually saying them and I can't concentrate on long questions. I am half-asleep as far as my face goes. Trudging back with my armful of mattress stuffing I get left far behind as I've forgotten about the wonderful brainwave scheme, and am side-tracked by a brown bird which runs nimbly head-first down a branch with its chestnut-coloured tail spread wide like a fan. Madagascar coucal, the size of a thrush. I never see thrushes in England nowadays. The crew come to collect me, dealing with me patiently like a deranged aunt, and steer me back to the Albert Hall. I bring out the length of sacking and spread it out on the rocks to cut it. Immediately parts of it fall into the puddles and rock pools, and I think also that to cut it may be a mistake. Once cut, it's cut, and there are days ahead when I may need a huge piece of sacking so I fold it over double and then over again. The plan is to sew down the two shortest sides and stuff the grass into the cavity to make a gaping duvet. Four thicknesses of sacking. This reminds me of my beautiful deserted A-frame, and as I push and drag the needle to and fro I am yearning for the A-frame across the island, standing free and wild on the open beach. Six stitches take a minute, 'and miles to go before I sleep'.

As always when I undertake some major task, the overtures to night start up. The light, dimmed already by familiar rain clouds, falls fast. Just in time, and out of bravado. I finish the tragic mattress, throw it on to the rock bed, and myself on to it, to show the crew, the camera, the world that it will be a night of bliss ahead. Even as I lie there, patting my handiwork and smiling, I can feel that it has been a hopeless exercise. The lalang stalks are clumped underneath my boasting attitude, if anything exaggerating the dismal hospitality of the stones. 'Well done', say the crew, and off they go, laden like Burmese mules with all their heavy valuable tripods and sound equipment and camera cases. When they turn away and head shipwards I feel abandoned. This is always the worst time – leaving. Before and after, I feel fine, but there's something really dreadful about

The crew watches me patiently as the mattress gets going. Each stitch takes a month and rainclouds are gathering.

leaving; trains pulling out, coffins going into graves, car doors slamming. When the crew have gone round Slippery Rock, I'm all right again and can watch them going slowly like refugees to the bobbing rubber boat. It's dark already and they have a lamp aboard. As they set off into the dark sea I run and get my big torch and wave and signal goodbye. A storm of biting insects covers me in seconds because I was still in my day wear, my bathing dress and shorts. How long will it take me to wise up? At night, from now on, regardless of heat, I will wear my long-sleeved shirt, trousers and socks. The shirt has become badly stained from the bites. When they brew up, they turn into watery boils and burst. It sounds foul but it happens so often to all of us that we have stopped even talking about it. The trousers stand up on their own. These things don't matter.

I've just realised that I haven't got any wood ready for the fire tonight. I'm going to cook another pathetic thumb-sized sweet potato and some rice and limes, but the wood situation is pretty grave, preparation-wise. The big torch, which I do my video pieces by, attracts moths the size of gypsies, and as I chip and tap away at the kindling I am dive-bombed and blithered by zooming night life. Big sticks aren't the problem – it's the beginning of a fire that matters. Some sticks split open to reveal a hurrying horde of woodlice or ants and, with Buddhist virtue, I lay that stick aside and help the anxious homeless to safety. An hour and a half later by my green watch, the black can is boiling and I toss in the potatoes, rice and the stock cube. As this is all there ever will be till the end of time, it's impossible to work up any curiosity or interest in supper. It's eating to live. How easily I'm shifting the tripod over the fire so the can reaches the flames. I swirl about in its dark, clanging, sloshing interior with my wonderful if too-large coconut ladle, but I can't see what I'm doing. Feed the fire, sharpen the knives, scratch the hair. I should make a comb, the kind Africans use, but it will take a bit of skill and time, both in short supply. The carrot resting in its perfect white clam shell has gone soft and a bit black. I wish I'd eaten it on the first day when it was fresh. I saved it, like a wise virgin, but it's hopeless now. Strange smell: the ladle sticks in the billy-can, the supper offering is burnt. I get my big knife to scratch the black and grey mass from the tin into my army mug. I use my cap as an oven glove, and squeeze three God-given yellow limes over the dark mess of pottage. It is, to be frank, grim. I bolt it down, chawing up scales of charcoal and, I think, rust. The vow is this: I will have to tell my crew of the sacred time before the sun goes down, when the Micks said you should eat. Drink in the darkness, but eat in the daylight. Every tiny problem is multiplied by ten without light. I must have time on my own before sunset.

In the evening in the cave I take off my bathing dress and go about fairly naked to try to dry off. My cloth sarongs are a boon, although quite often I just squelch about in the fish feet or cave shoes and nothing else, like a warning against taking Health and Beauty too seriously. Tonight I can feel through the sacking the sharp stems of the lalang grass and, to my lethargic despair, the brisk nips of some small biters who have travelled from Horseshoe Valley to be with me in the mattress. A great tranquillity suddenly overcomes me. Tonight I shall

After I finish drawing the little cricket, my back is covered with sandfly bites.

70

be bitten, lie scrunched up and awake, with the charcoal stew churning inside me, but tomorrow I will go. Dear cave, thank you for the shelter. I can stick it out tonight but this is the end. I don't care what happens to me tomorrow night but I shall sleep outside in the wind or rain, along with the raggle-taggle gypsies-oh. Before I settle down I anoint my back with Madame Lala's oil. There are bites there the size of egg cups; I think I got them when I sat to draw a cricket which was sitting on a lovely leaf on Sandfly Rise. I knew I was being bitten but if I moved, so would he. He waited patiently until I had drawn the last leg, then sprang off and away. This may sound a bit loopy, but I am beginning to believe that some of these creatures, birds, crabs, fish, understand me and are prepared to help. Fasten the white jacket behind my back but that's what I feel. They have looked into my eyes and their eyes are those of my own little cat at home. The insect's eyes are almost too small for this communication; but the fruit bat knew me, and so did the heron whose distant cousin steals fish from our London pond. My head is like a periscope, a pole supporting two eyes which are just windows through which my rambling invisible soul stares. My arms get hold of things and put me to bed. Buckle the white jacket tightly.

cricket on leaf sat just long enough for me to draw him

71

Day...

Dawn. Even though the cave faces west I can see something has changed in the early morning sky. Something looks completely different about the world outside. I can hardly get the fish feet on fast enough. Curving over North Beach and Marble Arch there are two tall rainbows and the sea is made of turquoise silk and long gold shadows are spreading over the rocks. It is quiet: no wind, no rain, no movement but the gentlest motion of the dreamy water. As it reaches the rocks it frills and gasps and withdraws. In its crystal clear deeps you can see down to the sand, two fathoms down. The sky is empty, the morning is blue and gold. It's 5.40 a.m. Everything is easy, I run like a cat on the rocks, dart into the cave like a lizard and in minutes a brilliant fire is blazing, the last breakfast tea in the cave will be drunk, I will pack and move when the crew comes, and they can carry things in their manly brawny arms round to the A-frame.

Just as the tea is ready I knock the whole lot over my leg. This doesn't depress me or even interest me. I'm going to make instead a lime cordial I have thought up. In India it is called *nimbu pani*. I measure half a litre of purified water into the clean billy-can (the burnt one is outside under the dripping rock; it makes me feel sick to look inside it) and cut up eight limes, squeeze their juice and throw

The most perfect coconut I've ever eaten. Having very little food makes you appreciate every mouthful.

. . . SIX

in the skins too. As it boils, I put in about two medium shells of brown sugar. I bartered my white sugar for brown, an excellent transaction as five sachets got me half a packet. I let the cordial boil for about ten minutes and then leave it to cool as I get washed and dressed. I wash anywhere, in puddles or under Shower Rock but it's a fairly cursory exercise. Then using a broken spiral shell as a funnel I decant the brownish cordial into the water bottle. It's now 6.10 a.m.

The crew usually aim to arrive at seven-thirty. I'm going to go off round the island and they can find me later. I'm going down North Beach through Marble Arch, round the small rocks to Shipwreck Beach. here in the middle of a tiny perfect cove is the upturned hull of a dinghy, almost covered with sand, like the husk of a coconut. This is a slightly longer but far prettier way round to Dolphin Beach. There's a rock here called Angry Old Man, sitting sulkily with his knees drawn up and a down-turned carroty nose. From here I can see the A-frame, just visible against the undergrowth. My heart is leaping and I am almost skipping along. On the beach as I climb down I can see something which looks like a slowly moving column of mice. Not crabs: can't be mice going down to the sea. Slowly, slowly I creep up on them. I am going to faint. I can't believe what I can see: ten, twenty, thirty baby turtles beetling along like little clockwork toys, stopping for a breather, then trundling on. I step amongst them carefully.

Shipwreck Beach – I wonder whose boat this was; the sand has nearly covered it. Behind are the smooth rocks where I slept out one night, and from where I watch the morning dolphins showing off.

They are all around me, travelling in unerringly straight lines, from the edge of the undergrowth to the receding sea. They are at most two inches across, dark brown with big front flippers and smaller hind ones. I pick one up and it continues to paddle in the air, opening its tiny little sand-covered black eye to look at me. I put it down and off it goes waddle waddle, stop for a breather, waddle waddle, like a clockwork mouse. The turtles are digging their way out from the buried shells, struggling out of sandy pits, alerted by the sound of the high tide, so now they must have been trundling down the beach for two hours. Sometimes one goes head-first into a crab hole and gets stuck, little back flippers waving. I dart about like a fairy tern, light and quiet as a feather, getting baby turtles out of the sandpits and following them down to the edge of the sea. As soon as they hit the water they stop for a second, then lesson B comes into action and they start

ABOVE **One of the most enchanting sights I've ever seen. The baby turtles will grow to the size of a coffee table.**
OPPOSITE **The Micks at Pirbright would forgive me for my weedy lashing – I love green army string but the twine I smuggled is even tougher.**

swimming strongly, putting their tiny noses up for air. Sometimes the first wave sends them back topsy turvy tumbling and they struggle and scramble their way on to their fronts and beetle off again. They swim straight out to sea. Forty, fifty, I can't count them all. Shall I keep one to show the crew? They'll die with envy. But I daren't. This must be the absolute time to dash from the hatchery to the sea and if I delayed one, that might kill it or change its life. But the crew! I haven't brought my drawing things or video camera. The last turtle is going. Just before he goes I pick him up to have a final look to impress him on my mind so I can do a scrappy drawing from memory. Small tortoise mouth, flat flippers, tiny brown back which will grow to mammoth proportions. By standing there I may have been their guardian angel as the herons and frigate birds couldn't get them. With any luck there will be an extra number of turtles this year. Brave little creatures! This is a present for me from the island to say all will be well. She did the rainbows and now the turtles and the perfect day. Everything has changed.

By the time the crew arrive we are all in terrific spirits. They're sad about missing the babies but what the heck! We're all swimming and planning what to do today and I've picked up some scorchingly lovely shells. I'm going to make the A-frame nice again; it's standing up remarkably well, so I make shelves at each end and do a bit more lashing. I'm trying to be economical with my army string but become hypnotized by the beauty of methodical binding. Paddy told me to do things neatly even if you're the only one who sees it, but the first lot was done in such an exhausted hurry that I can't get it to look Irish Guards-ish unless I undo it, which I won't on the premise of if it ain't broke don't fix it. I tie the bamboo window-box on, and hang all my damp cave-dimmed cloths on the cross-poles. They flutter like prayer flags, bright as an Indian bazaar.

Everything is put on the stretcher-bed and all the sand is shaken out and my treasured things are put in order. The mosquito net is re-hung, a canopy of white gauze dawdling over the bed. With twigs I sweep the Raymond Burrs which are the size of Maltesers and prickly as hedgehogs. Raymonds will continue to drop on to me from the tree over the A-frame. It's not a casuarina, as I asked the crew to look it up on the boat. It's called a local name, filaho. Now I'm barefoot again my feet will soon harden. At the moment Raymonds could get embedded in my white Plasticine feet. All the cuts will dry, the blisters will heal, the grazes will go.

Now I know what I need it's much easier to arrange things in order of importance. Always nearest your head, you knives and torch and, I suppose, the walkie-talkie. Also insect spray, drawing and writing things in the plastic bag, video camera, spare batteries ... hang on, this is ridiculous. Put everything at your head or feet and remember where they all are. It's like playing houses. At Mickledene School, where I started boarding when I was eight, we had an area under the dark fir trees called the Village. Each boarder had a House (there were only sixteen of us) and as the ground under the trees was bare of grass, we swept the earth and marked out our properties with pebbles and made cupboards in the roots of trees. Finding a forked stick, or half a brick, or a piece of string made all the difference to the decoration of your house. When everything was tickety-boo we'd invite each other in to have nettle tea. The happiness of man lies in the fewness of his wants. At the head of my bed I've put the piece of matting I made while I was a cave-dweller, a troglodyte, when? I can't remember days. I made it on my own, not out of the great green crisp palm leaf but from an old soft brown small one. It's ended up like a lattice-work sail and looks about perfect at the pillow end of the stretcher. There is no pillow but tonight I will roll a cloth

Tidying up the matting which I made from memory. My sarongs hang out to dry on the A-frame.

round my clothes and lie straight as a sentry on the excellent sacking. I am actually clucking with pleasure, my brain is hen-sized. We shall go off to cut down a coconut. I've seen this done but it usually includes an incredibly fit, young man with hardened feet and a parang or machete. All the coconuts I've seen seem to be miles high. The ones which have fallen in earlier cyclones are now bad, their watery insides reeking of alcoholic cesspools. Also I noticed that the fit young man had to slash and hack to get through the wrist-thick stem from which they depend. My little knife could cut through a brazil nut shell, but my big Anaconda knife from Germany defeats me when I try to sharpen it. It feels sharp against my thumbnail but then doesn't cut. I've tried doing it as I was shown, with a bit of the Acme coconut oil and my carborundum stone but I can't get the right angle on the blade. At home I have my penknife as sharp as a scalpel. The coconut expedition could end in a No-Film Misery situation.

It nearly does. They *have* to film me getting a coconut down, you can't be on a desert island and not cut and eat coconuts. Also, although food-wise I'm completely numb, the thought of a coconut is very appealing. We come to the selected tree. It looks as though the visiting fishermen, may their tribes increase, have chopped footholds into the trunk. I can't even begin to climb up. The coconuts are fifteen feet high. I get a long bamboo pole and start a sort of tossing-the-caber movement, nudging the nut, which hangs on unperturbed. They *must* film the nut as it falls. We struggle on, my utterly weedy arms bloodlessly manoeuvring the pole with softer and softer taps. Nothing will get this limpet down. So, reader, I send one of the crew up to loosen it. We were using up so much film – what else could I do? He twisted it gently and 'It's practically off already': down he shinned, camera turns over, bagwoman taps coconut with caber and it hurtles down like a bomb and cracks. I hold it up and from the Hallowe'en slit pour coconut juice into my face and neck and eventually mouth.

Hacking the top off the coconut isn't as difficult as I imagine. A good example of a sandfly bite can be seen on my left arm.

I've been told not to call it milk, and water it is not. This was coconut nectar. We all had some, then split the yellowing whiskery husk by jamming in the big blade. Inside the good sweet delicious meat was not yet formed. The coconut was frankly empty. But the juice was perfect and the film had got one of its vital ingredients. Near where the coconut grove stands are papaya trees. All the fruit seem to be bright green, and they are hanging up quite high. I've done with fruit collecting for today; anyway, what's the point of a unripe pawpaw if you're not hungry?

I escape from the crew and set off like a drug addict in search of shells. I can't explain how important they have become. Every single one is different, even shells of the same species. Nature has infinity in the palm of her hand, doesn't even try to impress. How many snowflakes have fallen in the history of the world? Billions upon zillions and yet no two have ever been found to be the same.

The water is translucent, diamond bright. As the waves break and suck back again you can see the jewels in the sand underwater. You pounce, rinse off the grains of sand and it might be the One, the shell we're all looking for. I collect

OPPOSITE **I see no ships: the pose of a person who has lost her marbles.**
BELOW **Filming with the crew round the A-frame, where they quite often dump their gear in the daytime.**

so many on every hundred-yard stroll that I can't carry them in my hands and have to tuck them into the body of my bathing dress next to my skin. I become the bobbly-body woman. When I empty them out at the A-frame I forget one or two which lurk like blue nylon goitres. My bathing dress is losing its elasticity and, unless I am getting much fatter, seems to be shrinking. I meant to wash the salt water out of my clothes and hair every day but that idea went down in seconds as it's far too much trouble and completely unnecessary. My head itches but I scratch it, so that doesn't matter. If you can't see yourself you simply cannot find it in your heart to give a pin how you look.

There's the fish eagle again wheeling around quite low down. I can see his white square-shaped tail and long finger-like wing feathers. The giant bird the Roc, which carried off Sinbad, came from Madagascar. For years people believed that this legendary bird was based on the *Aepyornis maximus*, the now extinct elephant bird, which couldn't fly. This was the only winged creature large enough to carry off a man; but it couldn't fly. There you are, they said, fairy stories. But the name of one of the principal tribal groups near the capital Antananarivo is called Voromahery, which means strong bird – and above the Queen's palace, on gateways and pinnacles, is the symbol of the royal family, a really colossal eagle, as big as the one on top of the American Embassy in London. Just an attractive mascot, they said, size exaggerated of course. Now, suddenly a

ABOVE **Dolphin Beach at its empty best. You can lose hours just walking and swimming.**
OPPOSITE **Beachcombing for nothing more than shells. My brain has shrunk to the size of the shell I'm holding up.**

Eating in a rather disgusting way. By this time I've forgotten what I look like which is just as well. Shell dish and spoon in action.

palaeontologist working in Madagascar has uncovered the bones of an enormous eagle, far larger than anything dreamed of in fables. This might just be the Roc. Extinct, of course. O Madagascar Fish Eagle, don't die out. Once I was taken to a trophy room in Pennsylvania: I thought it would be full of silver cups for golf tournaments but it was a hall filled with death, the heads of the rarest and most beautiful wild animals all nailed up, with a placard under each one saying where it had been shot. At least one of the deer I know now to be extinct. Who can these people be? What goes on in their heads? I didn't think all this as I watched the fish eagle, because when I'm walking and watching there is nothing but now, and no other place. I've found a rock on the beach which is high out of the water, so I put a collection of really good shells on it like a display cabinet. I grade them in size, rather than into patterns: spiral, clam, cylinder, flat, white, cowrie, speckly. The sun is booming down like a coppery gong. They can sit on the rock and bake in the afternoon sun.

The crew would like to film me eating supper. Oh. So I old-woman-foot it round the beach collecting biscuit-dry sticks, and prop up a tripod and smack together a tasty little fire, like a bushwoman. Same old rice, watery stock cube, test it using the ladle, slop it into the clam shell and try to eat tidily as I'm on camera. I think the crew feel sorry for me with my vegetable stock cube because when they've gone I find a mango on my bed. Someone had sneaked me a mango from their cruise yacht where they go back and tuck in in the evenings. I sit smelling it for ten minutes, then walk down and eat it in the sea as the sun goes down, all alone, waist high in sapphires, mango down my front, the stars just beginning to show. There is a scaldingly majestic sunset. The fruit bats who'd got a whiff of the mango come round in fours, very close, having a good look at this clever old bat who has scored a mango and who sleeps sideways instead of upside-down. Because there is no other light, no street lights, car headlamps, cities, ringroads, no light at all except for my miner's lamp flickering on the sand, the starlight is almost dazzling. There are stars you can't see from England (because here we're in the southern hemisphere, but also because there is no competing light). Drifts of stars, clouds of stars, glittering like diamonds.

Back at the A-frame, ready for bed, I can't stop staring at the sky. My neck is almost back to front. I don't want to be under the mosquito net which veils the stars. I get the mattress sacking, now emptied of all its grass, and walk off towards Shipwreck Beach. This morning I remembered, with a collector's eye, a large smooth rock. Nothing is frightening here. I can walk without a torch in the starlight, off the beach up on to the rocks and round to the smooth place where I will sleep. It doesn't seem that the high tide will reach me. I shall watch the stars all night long, and see if the moon appears. *Perchè tarda la luna*, sings the crowd in Turandot's court, why is the moon so late? And the chorus murmurs in anticipation – 'O pallid face, O silent one, come!' I can't quite remember that tune either.

Day...

The water is lapping at my hair and I feel as though I've been asleep in an aeroplane, stiff and crook-necked. The light is ashen grey and the stealthy sea has crept up on me on my rock. The sky is getting paler by the second. I was cold for a short time in my sleep, probably when a breeze got up on this little ledge and blew through my sacking. How nice to get up and find that you're dressed already. Les Quatre Frères, the tall sentinel islands called The Four Brothers, seem to have changed position and are either closer in or further from the shore, with their crowns of circling seabirds. Are they a mile away? Distance over water is very deceptive.

Under my rocks the small waves barely bother to move, just slopping to and fro sucking and sighing at the oyster rocks. There is a sudden smooth dark shape, then another, then they're gone. Out of the water only ten yards away burst the morning dolphins, twisting and jumping in pairs, swimming upside down. I can't count them; twelve or fourteen? Beyond me where the tide is coming up on Shipwreck Beach the dolphins tumble about in the surf. I climb on to an overhanging rock to get a better view and they bullet past underneath me, doing

ABOVE **Even while swimming the hunt for shells continues. The sea is twice as salty as the English Channel.**
OPPOSITE **The siesta in the A-frame. I am pretending to write my diary, but am in fact studying for the staff college, an old army phrase meaning falling asleep.**

. . . SEVEN

forty miles an hour, missing the rock by inches. When they surface I see their eyes watching me; the more I applaud the more they show off. Only after they've gone do I realise that I've missed my chance of swimming with them. I could have ripped off my trousers and shirt and socks and run round to the beach, and taken off my shoes and plunged in with them. Instead I stood here on the rock, turned to stone with excitement, and missed my chance. But if I had gone through all the palaver of undressing and negotiating the rocks they might have gone and I wouldn't have been able to watch them. These things I ponder as I make my way back to the A-frame.

Shell Rock, as I pass it, is empty of shells, the sea is surrounding it. The sea had given me all those beautiful shells and then last night it came and took them back. Sloshing around in the shallows, I find some of the bigger ones but the others have gone. This is a bit of a blow as I really loved those shells, those very ones. They were my best shells. I don't want other ones, I want those ones. If I hadn't been so greedy and collected so many I could have got them back to my camp. But it's impossible to feel gloomy in the perfect fresh bright turquoise dawn

light. Today will be blazingly hot again. I've stopped putting on the 25-factor sun cream as, when I go in the water or cool off under a water drip, it gets moist and looks like Ian Holm's head in *Alien*, slimy and whitish. There's no doubt though that it's laid the foundation for the excellent sun-burned skin I have now, my terracotta Miami leather skin. Now all I use is coconut oil and the sea. I am becoming invincible.

I am fiddling around at the A-frame when the crew arrive, already filming as they negotiate the exodus from the rubber boat into the waist-deep water. They were so pleased for me last night, leaving me to sleep at last on the stretcher bed in canvas-slung comfort, that I don't know whether I dare tell them that after all my carping and whining about the cave's hellish discomfort I chose to spend my first night of freedom on the rocks again.

The mosquito net, when I brought it in its green nylon sack, had a wooden attachment I haven't used, a set of wooden slats which are held together at one end by a butterfly screw, allowing them to fan out like the spokes of a bicycle wheel. Today I am going to make a parasol like Robinson Crusoe. His was made of goatskins, mine will be made of banana leaves. The crew will film this and the camera is turning over before I really think it out. Army string twined around the hub and a straight stick gives me the basic frame; but I am trying to do it far too fast, trying to *Blue Peter* it into shape, stitching and knotting and bluffing my way. The end result is pretty catastrophic, but held up to the light the banana leaves are a wonderful light apple-green colour and it looks quite pretty. I think I'm just doing things for the camera now, or there won't be a film. You can't film me mooning around and looking for my lost shells, or sitting and staring. You can't film

OPPOSITE **Even at this stage of construction I can tell that my umbrella is going to be a flop. I'm sunproof anyway.**
RIGHT **The finished item might catch on at Ascot.**

inside my head where changes are taking place as all you'd see is a completely normal healthy person in a catatonic trance. Cameras never see dirt; if you're in a television play which requires you to look slightly grubby you have to roll in sump oil and drag your clothes over coal dust before the camera notices the slightest fleck. On camera if you want to see rain you have to turn on water cannons. Most films where actors have hair clamped to their heads are shot in rain. Camera sees clamped hair, doesn't see rain, and with powerful lights it all looks like a sunny summer's day. Cameras lie, all the time. Only very skilled people or complete amateurs can get them to tell the truth.

As I haven't had any sort of breakfast, I'm off to see if there are any ripe pawpaws in the coconut grove. Nobody bothers to comment on Mosquito Alley any more; we cover up and trudge through. Journeys which seemed long and confusing are very simple now that we all know the island better. At the top of one papaya tree is an orange-coloured fruit. All the rest are green. I hadn't noticed the orange one before, when we came here last, but now I can't remember when that was. My mind is cartwheeling along; taking its feet off the pedals. I don't remember when we came because it's not important so my mind didn't keep hold of it. At home I have to remember so much that the house is full of lists and diaries and folders of information, and files full of folders. Here I don't even have to remember my name. I grasp the stem of the tree and go sh-shake and down plops the papaya. It's perfect, almost on the turn, but soft and ripe. Cut it open with the small knife, and inside there's that hot cinnamon-orange colour with jet black pips. We all have a mouthful and then I just stuff the rest into my face.

I've put in a request for an orange and an apple, and I filch cigarettes as often as I can.

The heat is ridiculous. If I were alone, I wouldn't be out in the midday sun. I would collect firewood early, eat before sunset, swim for three hours a day, collect shells till I turned into a hunchback and doze off every four hours. It wouldn't be a good film, day after day of that. So we head off to the Redout so I can be filmed drawing the islands and the shoreline.

Good grief, it *is* hot! I wish I had bothered to make some more lime cordial. The crew had some of that and said they liked it, although they didn't clamour for more. I have a feeling the sugary brown liquid would do us all some good.

Old woman legs are back with me again, and sometimes I stumble as I walk, tripping over my feet which are the size and weight of gun dogs. The crew are tired, too, their thoughts turning towards weightlessness in deep-sea diving gear. Sometimes they go diving when they go back to the ship for lunch, and return with tales of rays and coral and plump finger-sucking anemones. They're working so hard

OPPOSITE **Paw paws, or papayas, are orange when ripe: there will be a good harvest when I've gone. These green ones are white inside. Food doesn't interest me much now.**
RIGHT **Drawing is far more important. This is the view from the Redout – I'm trying to get the shoreline right.**
OVERLEAF **The crystal mattress.**

on this trip – when they leave at night, they have to check the stock, and write lists and clean the equipment, recharge and reload batteries and all day they cart the film gear around in the boiling sun.

The last slope up the sandy hill to the Redout nearly does for us all. The sun is directly overhead and I suppose the temperature is somewhere around 110 degrees. As I sit with my oil-stained drawing book on my lap I can feel the heat like molten iron, like an iron poultice on my bare back. I can't open my eyes in the glare. With my button compass I deduce that I am looking west north west, straight over this colossal stretch of water dotted with islands towards Mozambique. How did the early settlers have the stamina to get here? For they came not from Africa but from Indonesia and Malaya, all the way across the Indian Ocean to land on Madagascar. The language is Malay-based, mixed up with French. I suppose it's no stranger than European people living in Australia, but in Australia there were people already there, the Aborigines. In Mauritius and the Seychelles and in huge Madagascar, the fourth largest island in the world, there was no trace of human life before the Dutch and French and British and Indonesians came. They never bothered with Tsarabajina – even now the name is sometimes written Tsara*ban*jina, as though nobody had thought it worth recording accurately. Beautiful Sands, Belle Vue, Mon Repos, New Castle, Happy Valley: they're the same the world over, descriptions of the place, sometimes with a proper name attached; Williamsburg. Trafalgar Square, Leningrad. Ho hum. I have turned into a smouldering fossil. It's too hot to go on filming. The crew, unbelievably, are going to call it a day, and respect my wishes for solitude and early eating by returning to the boat now, at two o'clock. They leave me water and an apple, radio the rubber boat and zoom off round the headland.

As soon as the boat is out of sight, the great canopy of silence returns, the vast silence of sea and insects and the pied crows cawing. Off with my clothes, and with my bathing dress on my head to keep away the sun, it's back to Paradise in three easy strides, to the sea and the shells, and the prospect of doing some drawing.

Probably because of the high salt content, the sea supports you as if you are lying on a crystal mattress. You can lie on your back on the dazzling water with no effort, arms behind your head, legs floating, not sinking like motorway bollards as they do in the English Channel. With your ears under water you can hear the rasp and swish of the sand and shells. When you wade or swim you can see the fish flitting past your ghostly limbs, never touching, never leaving you. Would I fish? I suppose I would have to. But I don't think I'd know how to go about it. Tie the hook on the line and hold it. Pull it up when you feel a bite, kill the fish, put it on the fire on a stick. I look through the water at the fish round me. They're completely safe as far as I'm concerned.

When the island is empty except for me, birds are everywhere. Now as I walk on the hot sand the herons slowly flap above me, a beady eye on the water. By Shell Rock, I find three wonderfully pretty shells: but wait! I recognise them! The sea has brought them all back again, re-throwing them like dice with a great

Behind me at the far end of Dolphin Beach is Shell Rock where the sea took my best shells. I keep finding them again with each new tide.

Day.

Through the white gauze of the mosquito net I am watching them: a pair of doves, cooing and burbling quietly as they walk round under the A-frame, pecking the Raymonds and sifting through pine-needles. Shall I frighten them if I lift the net in slow motion? Slowly, slowly, don't breathe: but they just glance up at me, and go on with their foraging, completely unsurprised and unafraid.

I am wet through. It rained last night, nothing too tragic but enough to make me bring my valuable things into bed with me so I could protect them with my body. I lay on the video camera, the walkie-talkie, the torch, the diary, the drawing book and, rather pathetically, the knives, which are used to being wet but don't care for it. Over me I slung all my clothes and sarongs, but even so it was clammy-cold at about three-thirty. Just before the rain arrives there is a wind, like in the song 'Oklahoma' where the wind comes right before the rain. It gives you a warning of about forty-five seconds then blam! it pours. If you're asleep you don't hear or feel the warning. Last night's rain drove sideways so even the plastic groundsheet draped above the A-frame was no match for it. I've watched animals in fields, and ridden on ponies, in driving rain. Given the chance, they

ABOVE **Everyone who tries lying on the A-frame falls asleep as though they had been given a sleeping pill. I've stored some coconuts underneath – two were bad, as it turned out.**
OPPOSITE **The gorgeous fronds of the filaho trees shade the beach. I've rigged up the groundsheet in case of rain.**

. . . EIGHT

turn their backs to the weather and so did I, curled round my treasures. And after an hour it was all over, and when the wind drops you can build up a nice steam in your wet bundled huddle. Two hours of good sleep, and the gentle crooning of a pair of painted doves to take you to another day made of crystal and emerald: this is the life of the seraphim.

By the time I have hung all my wet things out to dry the crew have arrived, bringing a flask of hot coffee. Do they know that I'm too spaced out to bother with morning fires? The purified water from Shower Rock tastes like a municipal swimming pool, so I wait for their brilliant clear bottles of water. Yesterday I fell over very slowly like a camel; my head went empty and my loud voice said, 'Oh I'm going over' and in slow motion my legs gave way and I toppled over quite peacefully. I have become as weak as a puddle. Sometimes the effort needed to move is unbearable, but not unpleasant. My mind echoes like an empty saucepan. It's heat exhaustion brought on by not enough water and salt in my diet.

I want to show them my favourite walk on the island, past Angry Old Man and the rock where I slept, down on to Shipwreck Beach and into the rock canals

ABOVE **The army twine was just the ticket for this necklace. All the shells had holes in them already.**
OPPOSITE **This is the Lion Tree which became as comfortable as an armchair to me. Shortly after this picture was taken, I fell like a log to the ground from lack of water.**

under the Redout. It goes past Lion Tree, the bleached tree to lounge in on the beach, and doesn't go as far as Marble Arch, so you don't have to see the grey line of rocks leading to the Albert Hall. I'm collecting shells to make a necklace, broken spirals and shells with holes made by rocks or otherwise naturally, so today's search has an added frisson of excitement. I can't think what to give the crew as presents. Before I arrived I imagined myself making all kinds of elaborate small baskets and carved wooden ornaments but Old Father Time and Young Mr Film have put paid to that idea. There won't be time to find enough broken shells to make them all necklaces, and in any case the crew might see that as a bit girlie. But perhaps one shell each suspended on a nice bit of army string with their name and the island's name inside? I could write using my drawing pen. White shells, black writing, green string.

These are the happy dreams that occupy me as we dawdle down to the Lion Tree. On the way, I find easily, as if they had already been collected for me, five excellent shells for my necklace and four white ones for four of the crew. One shell clamours to be tried on. It fits my wedding ring finger perfectly; a dress ring, huge, bizarrely

shaped and exquisite. To my surprise the crew admire this ring and would each like to have one of their own. No amount of searching, however, turns up anything even remotely similar.

Why do I love one part of the island more than any other? It's to do with the shapes of the rocks, the natural way trees shade the sand, the smallness of the beaches, the rapid silvery rivers swirling in and out of the channels. It's because it has no memories of anxiety and sulking, no dripping rocks. At home there are journeys I don't like and will always go a different way, given the chance. There are some roads in East Kent that have a strangely menacing feeling even on hot summer days. When I first saw Stonehenge I couldn't get out of the car, I was so afraid. There is a hilly mount in Italy, somewhere between Florence and Siena, where a gory battle took place and when I went there all I could sense was shrieking and death and hatred, even though there were butterflies on the scratchy meadow grasses and high clouds in the blue sky. There are auspicious and evil places and it's important to know good from bad. You can only do this by opening up the inner ear, the one you keep turned off in traffic, when watching television and in crowds. We seem to have imposed a way of living on to places without first listening and looking. You can't just build places and make people live in them without knowing where the sun set and how the moon's light will fall. What will the people have to see? Will it give them a chance to see something good from their windows? Hundreds and thousands of years ago these things were of paramount importance to ordinary people but now we have imposed on top of the natural world false lights, false contours and motorways; we have denuded hills of their thick jungly coat so that the unstable soil slips away into the rivers, leaving bald mountain bones behind. How are we ever going to get back from this brink of the abyss? Hush, hush; here's another lovely shell.

I have to scribble things down as I walk, as thoughts fly by so fast and so lightly that it's like catching thistledown. I'm supposed to carry my rucksack with me but as I get lazier I leave it stashed under boulders or dangling from a tree. Madame Lala's oil has emptied itself spectacularly all over the inside, luckily only over my shirt and trousers. There is a way of making soap from ash and ... er ... potassium permanganate I think, but it doesn't seem worth the tremendous trouble. Swish the clothes about in the sea, hang them from the A-frame. If I were here for a long time I wonder if I'd be able to make a little boat or raft to get to the small islands. I could hollow out a tree trunk with the big Anaconda knife but it would take weeks. If I made it canoe-shaped I could balance it like a catamaran with poles, and it would be easier to steer than a raft. I'd never attempt to escape from here. Remembering the view from the helicopter, land is miles away and I'm scared of the sea.

I'm encouraged to have a go at opening a coconut with my knife. I've been dreading this. Haunted by dreams of cutting off my own hands, I have avoided chopping at anything which I have to hold. The first few blows are pathetic and the husk is far more resistant to the blade than I'd hoped. I've got to do it: the camera is running. Courage. Hack hack and then the clonk of striking the wooden shell through the fibre. Biff smash and we're through to the white meat and the glorious juice and really it wasn't so bad. It's just that I can hear the sound of the knife going through my wrist. Once at school I

RIGHT AND OPPOSITE **Getting more gibbon-like by the minute, all manners gone, I hack and guzzle coconuts. Once I stopped being afraid of using the big knife, cutting things became easier.**

was sent a block of brittle toffee. Dividing it up in the washroom, I stabbed the blade of my penknife through my fingernail and through my finger. The pain was excruciating but it's the sound that lingers in the memory: a thudding scrunch. If that hadn't happened I wouldn't be afraid of knives. If those joking boys hadn't blocked off the end of the watery underwater tunnel in the swimming pool in Malaya just when my lungs were bursting, and I had to push and push at their legs and then turn and make my drowning way back the way I came – if that hadn't happened I would still love swimming. As it is I can hardly stand under a shower without panic arising, and I won't do the crawl, haven't from that day to this, because you have to put your face under water. I was taught to swim when I was three but now I don't care much for swimming and get out of it whenever I can. Lolling, lazing, dowager duchess breast-stroke, fine: but diving,

ABOVE **Setting up this shot for the film crew took so long that, by the time I dived in, the water had reached my waist. The sea is full of beautiful exotic fish, invisible here.**
OPPOSITE **Preparing kindling takes ages and is extremely enjoyable. If I prepare enough, lighting a fire is child's play.**

not any more thank you; no more pretending to adore swimming.

And now we are walking to the other end of Dolphin Beach where there are shoals of fish by the rocks, and an underwater camera, which will look up at me through the briny deep as I peer down mesmerised by the ocean life. I perch on lava daggers which are as hot as a barbecue spit, on the oyster slashing rocks and the dry and wet cameras have me in a pincer view. There will be no escape: I must do a graceful schuss into the water, keep my head under and open my eyes. In the event it's not a problem, the salt water doesn't sting, I do some Esther Williams type movements and, like all dreaded moments, once it's over it seemed rather fun. Maybe it is as easy as this to get over a lifelong fear.

The rock pools at this eastern end of the island are very deep. Shafts of sunlight glint into them from strange underwater angles, a whole world going on out of

At first I thought it was a pineapple. The cycad's leaves are like leather straps.

sight under the hot-plate rocks. As the tide rises, the way round to Death Rock is fairly perilous. I clamber on, past a lush little valley full of huge pineappley ferns called cycads, one of the oldest species of plant known on earth. They only grow in this protected valley on the island: probably the soil and the protected position afford exactly the right requirements, and there must be a water source somewhere here although the vegetation is so thick that it would take an hour to hack a six-foot inroad to find out.

Death Rock is separated by a narrow neck of yellow sand, an isthmus marked by a single palm tree which leads to this high rocky island. Before we came we made a solemn promise to the king who owns these islands that we would never go to this part. I called it Death Rock because there is a local custom to bring dead bodies from the islands in the Mitsio Archipelago to this island, and to lay them to rest in caves on the easternmost point of Tsarabajina. After a year or so, when all that is left is a skeleton, the people return to collect the bones, wrap them in a clean cloth and bring them back to their village to be shown the changes that have taken place since the spirit passed over. They are introduced to new babies, shown new buildings and taken to look at the crops. This keeps the departed in touch with the world they have left behind. After that they are brought back to rest in peace in their cave on Death Rock. The fish eagle often flies above the cliffs here and as I stand on Palm Beach I wonder if anyone would find out if I sneaked over to explore. The spirits would know at once, I suppose, and might be angry. They might follow me back to London and come to tap on the cold windows on autumn evenings and rattle their bony fists at me. Come away, come away from Death Rock and idle down Shell Beach where the hermit crabs jostling on the dark sand make it almost impossible to walk. There must be something here that they love to eat. They have grown huge, clattering and staggering about with giant pincers in shells two sizes too small. Some of the shells are extremely lovely and to me in my rabid state most desirable, but I don't manage to get even one off a hermit crab. They fence back at me with clacking claws and reject the alternative shells I offer as a swap.

Suddenly the thought of the mango brings on an appetite. Even going quite quickly, I find that I've taken three-quarters of an hour to travel about five hundred yards, stopping and dreaming and losing my thread. In the rock cupboard I see that a bird has got here before me and with its beak, zrew zrew zrew, it has made inroads into the mango, deep slicing pecks. This will have been one of the pied crows, who follow me around at a distance, shouting the odds and hopping along in huge exaggerated bounds. I haven't managed to draw one as they never keep still. They go down to pick over small crabs in the surf, leaping to safety when the waves threaten to wet their toes. When I left my drawing things on the beach, with the objects that I was drawing, they descended to have a good nose round and scoffed down a tiny fish I was sketching which had been dropped by a gull.

I am thinking of home, of my family and my people, but now they're floating in a soap bubble, perfectly clearly seen but detached from me, as though they are on a neighbouring planet. I feel as though my boat has drifted away from the shore. I can hear myself breathing again, always a bad sign. Drink some water, woman, you're rambling. The crew are saying goodbye, and reminding me that this is my last night on the island.

So soon! But I have been here for months. I shall make the grandest fire yet, a bonfire on the open beach. Moving on, packing, preparing to go – all these heart-jumping things in store! The crew have already made a pile of wood for me and left an orange and a bottle of fresh water. There could not be a kinder crew in the world. It may rain again tonight but that holds no anxiety for me. I am the woman of the beach, a firemaker, a walker in darkness.

I stand in the water to watch the sun go down, my billy-can already boiling on the bright fire whose yellowness makes the blue beach even bluer. Phosphorus is back again in the water and on the beach. When I stamp on the wet sand sparks fly out. Last time there was phosphorus there was a storm. I wonder if the weather is changing again. It won't change before I go, I'm certain of that.

Into the black bubbling cauldron I toss the last of my rice, a whole stock cube and a squeeze of lime. The cooking time allotted is perfect – a grain bitten in half reveals a pinpoint of white. There was not too much water; I have made a lime rice risotto which is almost unbearably delicious. On to the fire I fling all

Sharpening the Anaconda knife, is best done in the daylight. I never managed to get it as sharp as Paddy would have liked.

the dried coconut husks I can find, and branches and bits of bamboo and dried seaweed stalks. Feed the fire, the flames leap up, the night air is violet and black, and the sky's dark clouds are moving in for the kill. I run barefoot on the beach in the dark. My night eyes can now see easily, twigs and wood, even in the shadows. Burn, fire, burn. I remember the demon Army matches which I haven't used, those would burn brightly ... but wait. Don't waste anything; leave a present for the next person who may arrive here, leave the Army matches or better still the Irish Guards tin with the things I haven't used: the fishing hooks, potassium permanganate, needle, safety pins, my lovely little compass. The coconut husks burning keep the insects away and I sit by the fire writing as though my hand will drop off.

My last night on my desert island and what have I achieved? Yes, I've survived but there was never going to be any doubt about that – the BBC could hardly put me on an island and leave me to die. There was always the crew and when they weren't here there was the walkie-talkie. I had rice and begged for fruit. I made things: some hugely successful, like the cave shoes and the coconut ladle and my necklace, and some not so terrific, like the umbrella. Would anyone want to spend their life quite alone, I wonder. Not I: I love people and I love all the complicated and sophisticated things people achieve, like piano concertos, the Sistine Chapel, Indian take-aways, gardening catalogues. But what I have been allowed here is something more precious than platinum and that is solitude. It took a very short time to let go of the world outside, but when it had gone I felt completely at peace with myself. The truth is all of us do so many things we don't want to every day, hear so many terrible bits of news, are affected by so many other people, in advertisements, newspapers, streets, towns, shops, that we haven't got time in our heads to have a chance to think a single original thought. We are always reacting, with agreement or fury, to other people's ideas and it seems almost impossible even on holiday to shut out the clamour of other people's making. We're like the sea birds on Les Quatre Frères, squabbling and treading on each other; but unlike the sea birds we never get the chance to lift off and fly

in the huge quiet sky. Now I have been alone with myself for eight days (is it eight?) I am less afraid than I've ever been of the notion of not being alive any more. I have my own treasured belief that we are being watched out for, and that if you are going in roughly the right direction the path will be brightly lit. While the fire is still blazing, I shall make the shells ready for the crew's necklaces. In the firelight it's easy to see to write and the ink dries immediately. Sheet lightning is flaring on the horizon, and the thunder rumbles.

I tidy my things into the stretcher-bed, but I can sit by the fire for much longer as I know that a warning will be given – the wind which blows across the beach before the rain comes down.

Coloured tangerine by the setting sun, I decide to deliver the evening broadcast dressed in cave shoes and shell necklace, like Wilma Flintstone.

The thought of packing woke me before dawn. I am lying in the half-light with the sides of the mosquito net draped over the top of the canopy, like a humble four-poster bed. The net has become dark with needles from the filaho tree. I am listening to soft sounds of the surf bubbling and crawling on the glassy beach. Today is going to be a scorcher.

I have so little to pack that I don't want to start too soon, I want to savour each moment of packing up the nylon rucksack, whose very intense false blue has begun to fade into the colours of the sea. What shall I do about the A-frame? It is so phenomenally comfortable that it would be criminal to dismantle it. The fishermen when they next visit might get up and lie on it, as I have seen members of the crew doing from time to time. It has a sleep aura about it, you fall asleep almost at once, slotted like a papoose between the narrow poles. There is a great craze for huge beds, around which you can scuttle, king-size, emperor beds, but I prefer a narrow iron cot. The best beds were at school. Two-foot-six wide (like the A-frame) with sagging springs and a thin mattress: once you were in there was no option but to sleep, and if you tucked yourself in really tightly like a banana fritter you didn't even move. All this room in beds makes your unconscious dreaming body search

> **Impossible to choose which shells to leave behind. I must have collected a hundredweight, so some must go. I hate the idea of never sleeping in the A-frame again: I dread leaving its narrow bony security. Maybe I'll make one in England.**

...*NINE*

around for edges. When people twig how easy A-frames are to build (for two men) they will replace hammocks which are fairly treacherous inventions. As the materials used are completely natural, sacking, wood, string, my A-frame will moulder away if the fishermen don't want it. Or: the fishermen may undo it and keep the string, sit on the sacking and put their fish on the poles again.

I have collected far, far too many shells and the crew will not allow me to bring them back as we were already very overweight when we flew out. I am making piles of must keep, should keep, can throw out, sitting on the ground at the foot of my bed when the crew arrive. They look in very good shape. Some of them have had their shirts ironed on the pleasure steamer. Down comes the mosquito net as the camera whirrs, the Raymonds are picked out, the frothy white wedding veil is twisted and stowed away in its green nylon case. That will come home with me: it can be suspended from a nail and draped over a doorway, window or bedhead. I save my butterfly cloth for my going-away outfit and use all my other clothes to wrap around the shells. There are shells in bags, in socks, in leaves. I know them all, when and where I picked up each one. I give back the tripod, the video camera, the batteries, these are no longer my responsibility. Grief! There is almost nothing to pack. My palm leaf mat will not survive the journey so that will stay at the head of the bed. The banana leaf umbrella, collapsed and flabby, went on to the fire last night. The cave shoes, rinsed in the sea, dried in the sun, will come back to England – 'washed by the rivers, blest by the suns of home'. Drawing book and diary: packed.

Now, using first my big knife and then my hands, I dig a deep hole. The sand is dry here, beside the sandflies' repose under the filaho tree, dry even quite deep down. If I'd had to dig for water, letting it filter in a deep hole, collecting each precious drop and boiling it all, what a different film this would have been. I would have been lying on my face all day, sucking up moisture through a straw. Here is my SAS survival handbook falling open naturally at the chapters on tropics and poison; here is my dear Irish Guards tin with the lid tightly fitted back on. I have taken out the pills that I never used, aspirin, immodium and antibiotics. If someone found them they wouldn't know what they were for, as they have come in unmarked plastic sachets. Even I don't know which is which. I have written out a message:

> From Girl Friday to the next survivor on Tsarabajina. I, Joanna Lumley, leave you the SAS survival guide and the remains of my Irish Guards survival tin. Here also is an excellent recipe you may like to cook up in these tins: 2 chopped sweet potatoes, 1 handful of rice, $\frac{1}{2}$ pint purified water (tablets in the tin). Boil the above for fifteen minutes and serve drenched in the juice of fourteen limes. Serve on a clam shell. Joanna.

That goes into the clean billy-can with the Irish Guards tin and the book; the black-burned sickening scarred billy-can is rammed on top, to form a semi-waterproof canister, and I push it into the pit and start scooping sand over it. It is a strange and final moment. We are all silent. I remind myself of my cat, carefully clawing the soil from each side and patting it down.

All tiredness has left me. Strength has returned, I feel quite normal. One more walk around the island, leaving the best part till last. One last chance to see if my map is accurate enough as far as the coastline goes. I know why it's so exciting today. First I am leaving, packing, travelling, the dogs bark, the caravan moves on. Second, I shall be back with people again, and not stuck with only my own head for company. On all the travels I have been on in recent years I have kept diaries and journals and they're full of observations about life around me, people I meet, their customs and dress, what they eat, what their houses are like. The fascination of travel is in places, certainly, but best of all in the people. To be in a place without history is extraordinary. Here, there is no language, so my

---

The letter, survival book and Irish Guards tin are just about to be buried in the billy-cans. After I cover the hole I forget to mark the spot, so the chances of this treasure ever being found are slim.

language will do. There's no architecture, no costume, no religion, no type of cooking – there is nothing here but the fish eagles, fruit bats, turtles, crows, herons, doves, crabs, dolphins (the island cat never appeared). For nine days I have belonged to the island and been made to feel welcome; I haven't been a stranger, because I am the only one, but if I had the chance to stay on, would I? Would I? Try this test: you have to stay for another four weeks, how do you feel? Very terrible. I have geared the whole trip to knowing that I am getting away from this Tsarabajina, where my food has run out and where, without my back-up, I would have had a pretty thin time of it. It hasn't exactly been a fat time of it, but there was a shape to it, the rainy days and starry nights, the sun and wind and the swimming with fish.

I remember going to a party with my sister when I was about six years old. We both hated parties, and when the time came to be collected we overdid the praise and thanks out of relief, and our friend's mother said, 'Oh how nice, you've enjoyed yourselves, you CAN STAY ON and SPEND THE NIGHT'. And we cried out, 'Oh no! Oh no!' and ran to the car. Don't make me stay on the island any more. I am longing, with a longing I've kept hidden away, buried like my billy-cans, to sit at a table with friends, to eat lettuce, to be at home. As I say these things in my head or out loud, a wave of remorse comes along and nearly knocks me down. What am I? Am I any good at this survival, or am I an absolutely tame zoo animal, so conditioned to life in the Western world that my simple palate has become greedy for more; more complex, more intricate, more abundant, just more? No, it's not that. It's back to human company; not riches or the soft life which have never held much appeal for me, but the companionship and exchange of ideas with my dear beloved fellow human beings 'the glory, jest and riddle of the world'.

I am climbing round the great hunched rocky toad-back of the island now, revisiting all the places I thought I'd see every day, like the Jacuzzi and Heron Rock. Field glasses would have been a stupendous luxury, and a camera. I would have liked to have taken a panoramic view, taking a photograph and moving it along evenly, another one, move it along so that when you have them developed you can stick them overlapping side by side and say, 'There! That's what I saw', and watch your friends' eyes glaze over with indifference. These things will never mean anything to anyone else, that's another thing I've learned. Faces, views, animals infinitely beautiful to each one of us can't transmit the fascination to a casual observer. This is the whole attraction of trying to act out stories: trying to make the audience see things through the same eyes. That's why actors go on acting. Not for fame or money (though they have their place) but for the moment when you know you have the audience with you and they are thinking with your head. My black shadow, like fallen underpants, sculls along around my ankles, soaped into position, stitched on by Wendy. The sun is silently roaring down on the rocks. The heat is yelling, the island is trying to burn us away.

The Albert Hall is just around the corner. Where the tide has filled the

OVERLEAF **Before committing them to the ground the billy-cans are washed in a sea which is just getting rougher, a sign that more bad weather is on its way.**

pockmarked rocks with puddles they glitter as gaily as carnival flags. It will be all right now to go back into the cave. Since I left, I have turned my mind away from it. I loved it so much at first and then grew to hate it so violently that I feel bad about seeing it again. Here it is; just a cave, with a few of my sticks lying around, a bit of grass, three or four shells (I'll take those). The ceiling is blackened from the smoke. One day someone may come round here and say 'Look! We could build a fire here – someone else has', but mine was the first fire. Might even be the last, as the fishermen wouldn't bother to trek over to these devil rocks when they have the silken sandy beaches. I sit on my bed rock and look out of the Lion's Lips to Byron's Grave and the Scottish Castle. As I leave, so will their names, evaporating in seconds like water in a fire. The turquoise sea is almost impossibly bright, sparkling and dazzling. I never saw one ship or boat here. There was never even one aeroplane in the sky. How tame it will all seem, even in places like Fiji or the Seychelles, swarming with aircraft and vehicles. Where is wild any more? How dull a seaside villa will seem in comparison with the Albert Hall in a storm. How dull; and yet how attractive and comfortable and safe! And yet how dull. I shall miss having air all around me, shall hate having a roof overhead and stuffy walls and carpets and locked doors. How on earth will it be possible to read newspapers gain? Chatter chatter, on and on, skirts short or long, who's in or out, two points on the Dow Jones, busy busy like tricoteuses clacking their knitting needles as the heads roll. Is this what you miss, beachwoman, are you sure you love it so much? (Is this the island speaking?)

I can see that the rubber boat has pulled in and the crew are preparing to leave. I run like a lamplighter over the midday shadows, for the first time my feet as sure as crabs' claws. I am sprinting past Fat Man Rock, up Sandfly Rise, through Mosquito Alley, going too fast to be stung. The pied crows are wheeling and settling to watch the activity. The boat has to make several trips to the big ship and back, taking away with it each time a little bit more of our mechanised

Going down to the sea for almost the last swim on the island.

world. Chin deep in the hot green water I watch them bobbing away out of sight, we're all waving, we will all be together again this evening on another far away island, with a bottle of wine and candles and food on plates. There: they've gone. I'm going to swim and swim now, store up this feeling of bliss, of drumming heat and the empty beach. There are some new bites on my arms and one giant one on my shin. Some of the cuts round my ankles seem to be healing, but I couldn't really care less. My bathing dress has completely lost its grip now, making only the vaguest attempt to stay in position – where it has covered me I am as white as an almond, greeny white under the water with arms as brown as a tinker. My hair which I haven't thought about for days is not only still growing on my head,

OPPOSITE **Even at this late stage I've managed to grasp another shell. The crew are just about to leave ahead of me.** BELOW **Suddenly, when you're going to leave for ever, sand gets in your eyes.**

it feels springy and soft like a spaniel, completely undamaged – in fact, cured of its former ills. Put the fish feet in the rucksack, tie the butterfly sarong round my waist, buckle on the knives. I shall sit out here in the boiling sun dreaming till the helicopter eventually comes to collect me. But here it is already, and my heart contracts. Here it comes, too soon, droning like a hornet. I run to the trees, holding my cloth over my face till it lands, then in all the flying sand and roaring chopping water there is no time to say goodbye, only run to the open door, it's too loud to think, stuff the rucksack under a seat, smiling, yelling, 'Yes, yes, fine' and struggling to climb in because my legs are shaking, and slam the door, and as I am fumbling about with the safety belt we rise up and start wheeling away and we've gone before I had time to say goodbye.

Quotes

When I got back to London, I looked up some of the poems that had flitted in fragments through my brain. They weren't always appropriate, but something – usually one word – made that phrase or verse leap into my mind.

'Rage, rage against the dying of the light' (page 46) was written by Dylan Thomas. It comes from the exquisitely painful poem about his father's death, 'Do not go gentle into that good night'.

Having studied *Julius Caesar* by William Shakespeare for 'O' level English, it's not surprising that chunks of it are still with me now.

> *'O mighty Caesar! Dost thou lie so low?*
> *Are all thy conquests, glories, triumphs, spoils,*
> *Shrunk to this little measure?'*

cries Mark Anthony when he first sees his beloved Caesar's dead body lying on the floor, gaping with the assassins' stab wounds. Obviously it's got nothing to do with digging up potatoes (page 51).

Sir Henry Newbolt's poem 'He fell among thieves' is the thrilling and awful story of a man captured on the North West Frontier after a skirmish in which he killed five of the enemy for which he must pay with his life. He begs to be allowed to die in daylight, and spends his last night remembering his happy life in England. I quote this verse as it seems to evoke a perfect moment – the warm air, the scrunch of the waiting horses' hooves, the buzz of bees in the wistaria (page 54).

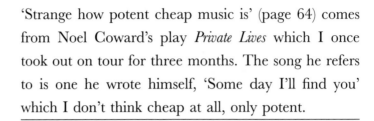

'Strange how potent cheap music is' (page 64) comes from Noel Coward's play *Private Lives* which I once took out on tour for three months. The song he refers to is one he wrote himself, 'Some day I'll find you' which I don't think cheap at all, only potent.

The American poet Robert Frost wrote the poem 'Stopping by woods on a snowy evening'. The last verse is:

> *The woods are lovely, dark and deep,*
> *But I have promises to keep,*
> *And miles to go before I sleep,*
> *And miles to go before I sleep.*

There is suddenly something absolutely frightening in the repetition of that last line: something which makes you want to shake the reins and drive on home without turning around (page 68).

Rupert Brooke's poem 'The soldier' which starts, 'If I should die, think only this of me:' is one of great peace and forgiveness – a celebration of gentle things, and of England (page 115).

I tried to learn the whole of Alexander Pope's *An Essay on Man* but failed. In Epistle II, he dwells on the combination in mankind of sweet reason and cruel arrogance, of man's power and his frailty (page 119):

> *Great lord of all things, yet a prey to all;*
> *Sole judge of Truth, in endless Error hurl'd:*
> *The glory, jest and riddle of the world!*